REGIONAL PLANNING

REGIONAL PLANNING

Evolution, Crisis and Prospects

Edited by
GILL C. LIM

ALLANHELD, OSMUN Publishers

ALLANHELD, OSMUN & CO. PUBLISHERS, INC.

Published in the United States of America in 1983
by Allanheld, Osmun & Co. Publishers, Inc.
(A Division of Littlefield, Adams & Company)
81 Adams Drive, Totowa, New Jersey 07512

Library of Congress Cataloging in Publication Data
Main entry under title:

Regional planning.

    Bibliography: p.
    Includes index.
    1. Regional planning—United States—Addresses,
essays, lectures.   I. Lim, Gill C., 1946–
HT392.R418   1982   361.6′0973   82-13839
ISBN 0-86598-097-7

83 84 85 / 10 9 8 7 6 5 4 3 2 1

Printed in the United States of America

Contents

Acknowledgments

This work attempts to bring together the most recent ideas about the evolution, challenges and prospects of regional planning in the United States. Most of the papers in this volume were first presented at the Conference on Regional Planning sponsored by the Woodrow Wilson School of Public and International Affairs of Princeton University in October 1981. Participants consisted of academicians, practitioners, and citizen representatives who share expertise and a deep interest in the subject. Many of the papers are studies which are based upon insights gained from practicing professionals. Subsequent to the conference, the papers were revised and the introductory and concluding chapters were added.

A number of people contributed to the organization of the conference and to the editing of this volume. The support and participation of Dean Donald E. Stokes is appreciated. Acknowledgment is due the graduate students of the Woodrow Wilson School who took part in organizing the conference; Brian Boxer, Dawn Boyer, Charles Cameron, Kathryn Duke, Carol Gossett, David Kodner, Paul Teske, Amy White, and Steve Williams spent many hours in planning and executing the conference. A special word of appreciation must be given to Dawn Boyer, Kathryn Duke, and Amy White who played key roles in running the conference. Brian Boxer, David Parker, Kathryn Duke, David Bernstein, and James DeMocker assisted in the editorial process.

The faculty and staff members who served on the Advisory Committee for the conference also played a vital role. Thanks are due Nancy Beer, Curtis Berger, Michael Danielson, Jameson Doig, Edwin Mills, Richard Nathan, Chester Rapkin, Ingrid Reed, Richard Roper, Jerry Webman, and Julian Wolpert. In particular, Professors Doig, Nathan, Roper, and Webman took valuable time to moderate sessions of the conference.

Laura Salant and Pat Stefanick have been instrumental in overseeing the manuscript preparation. Hannah Kaufman of the Princeton University Computer Center gave her time and expertise generously to the publication of this work. Finally, Anne Klein provided not only her excellent administrative support but also many valuable editorial suggestions.

G. C. L.

PART ONE

Introduction

1. Regional Planning in Transition

Gill C. Lim

INTRODUCTION

A quest for an appropriate framework for regional planning has continued throughout this century. The search has been accompanied by persistent conceptual debates concerning the fundamental justification for regional approaches to planning, and at the same time, by a phenomenal and steady growth in the number and variety of regional planning activities. Indeed, during the last decade or so, regional planning has become an important consideration in nearly all areas of public sector decision making about resource allocation. The extensive development of institutional mechanisms for regional planning that has taken place in recent decades is a result of both encouragement by the federal government and the voluntary efforts of local entities.

Recently, however, questions concerning the effectiveness of regional planning have brought certain agencies under critical examination. Their organizational efficiency and their ability to achieve stated objectives are under scrutiny. Following this evaluation of their performance, alternative roles for these agencies may evolve.[1] Furthermore, at both the local and national levels, important shifts in the political and economic environment demand a

3

careful assessment of the contributions and functions of regional planning. At the local level, the movement toward tax limitation and expenditure cuts, which began in recent years with Proposition 13, has substantially reduced local incentives to participate in regional planning efforts. At the federal level, the economic policy pursued by the Reagan Administration signifies drastic alterations in the fiscal relations between the federal government and the states and localities.[2] Current federal policies, designed primarily to facilitate the recovery of the national economy, call for almost complete withdrawal of federal support for regional planning.

The current shifts in local sentiment and in federal policy will trigger crises for most of the institutions engaged in regional planning activities. These shifts presage a significant and lasting impact on almost every regional planning agency in the nation. Pessimists contemplate that the changes taking place now will bring many regional planning agencies to the edge of dissolution. This may signify an intensification of the interjurisdictional conflicts and substantial costs to the nation due to the abandonment of valuable institutional resources. On the other hand, some critics contend that the rhetoric of regional planning has not been matched by its performance and that the current shift renders an opportunity to dismantle inefficient organizations. Only the most effective agencies will survive the crisis.

The collection of papers in this volume is addressed to the major issues currently facing regional planning. It is concerned with assessing the past contributions of regional planning, evaluating the immediate impact and long-term implications of current policy shifts, and seeking a suitable role for regional planning in the changing environment. This introductory essay discusses relevant conceptual issues, provides a working definition of regional planning, describes institutional developments in regional planning in a broad framework, and outlines the scope and plan of the volume.

CONCEPTUAL DEBATE: DECENTRALIZATION VERSUS INTEGRATION

Political decentralization, with important powers of collective decision making bestowed on local governments, is one of the unique features of the American political system. In most other countries, with the exception of some of the Western democracies, local governments have little autonomy and function mainly as administrative branches of the central government.

In many ways, the American system of federalism reflects the political values cherished and nurtured by the people. The founding fathers distrusted the centralized political system of European countries and carefully guarded against the concentration of power in one hand (Hartz, 1955). During the early years of the post-Independence period, deTocqueville (1838) observed that the advantages enjoyed by American local institutions were among the foremost reasons cited by its citizens for the country's power and prosperity.

Nowhere in the Constitution, however, are the rights or functions of local government prescribed.[3] Local governments are permitted to exercise those powers not possessed by the federal government and which are granted to them by the states and the people. Thus, the power to establish local institutions is derived from two important sources: the states and the people.

The institutional flexibility inherent in the constitutional framework has allowed social values and historical accidents to play a role in shaping the American political landscape. Political fragmentation was not a prevailing phenomenon in American urban areas until the third quarter of the nineteenth century. During most of the century, expansion of the cities was followed by annexation, creating larger, single jurisdictions. The period of annexation came to a halt, however, with attempts by the suburban areas to gain political autonomy and to separate themselves from the central city. Danielson (1976) notes that the objective of suburban separation originated from the conflict among classes and ethnic groups and reflected the desire of the middle-class population to maintain and to control the homogeneity of their communities.

Under these circumstances, local governments proliferated during the latter part of the nineteenth century and have remained as important units of public decision making in the twentieth century.[4] The historical data presented in Table 1 show that the total number of governmental units reached 115,116 in 1942. Since 1942, the reduction in the number is due mainly to the decrease in the number of school districts. In the meantime, special districts have almost tripled. The number of all other units has remained virtually unchanged. As of 1977, there existed 79,913 governmental units in this country.

Political values, social conflicts, and historical accidents have all contributed to the complicated and often confusing picture of territorial fragmentation which now exists. The magnitude of geographical fragmentation in a contiguous space is well illustrated by a typical metropolitan area. In 1977, there were 27,869 governmental units in 277 SMSAs. Twenty-three of these SMSAs had at least 250 units of government. Critics have maintained that the high level of political decentralization and territorial fragmentation led to considerable interjurisdictional conflict and limited the public sector's ability to deal with issues having significant welfare implications. Thus, many plans for integrating systems of governmental activities have been proposed.

TABLE 1

NUMBER OF GOVERNMENTAL UNITS

	1942	1957	1967	1977
United States	1	1	1	1
States	48	48	50	50
Counties	3,050	3,047	3,049	3,042
Municipalities	16,220	17,183	18,048	18,862
Townships	18,919	17,198	17,105	16,822
Special Districts	8,299	14,405	21,264	25,962
School Districts	108,579	50,446	21,782	15,174
Total	155,116	102,328	81,299	79,913

Source: U.S. Census of Governments, Various Years

Attempts to bring the government's operation and spatial configuration under a single integrated entity are justified on the bases of efficiency and equity. First, it is suggested that due to substantial scale economies in the production of public services by integrated units, the cost to the public is less than when the services are provided by fragmented local jurisdictions. Second, it is argued that local public goods can be delivered more effectively on a regionwide basis. Third, some suggest that it is necessary to have an integrated decision-making unit in order to internalize all interjurisdictional externalities. Fourth, an argument is made that a regional approach to public decision making facilitates the exchange of information and coordination among subunits within a region. Fifth, it is suggested that integrated systems of local governments can reduce fiscal disparities among its subareas. Sixth, some proponents of an integrated regional system argue that it can serve the goal of income distribution more effectively than can a fragmented system.

Available theoretical and empirical evidence is neither consistent nor overwhelmingly supportive of these arguments. Regarding the issue of scale economies, for example, existing empiricial studies show that average unit costs for electricity, gas, and sewage services decline with size, but are almost uniform or do not indicate substantial scale economies for education, police protection, fire services, and refuse collection (Hirsch, 1968). It is now generally accepted that per capita public spending increases with city size (Peterson, 1976). Some theoretical analyses of local decentralization, such as Rothenberg (1970), have demonstrated that jurisdictional fragmentation results in suboptimal use of resources in the public sector. However, Bradford and Oates (1974) have shown that although an integrated system of local government can lead in the long-run to a somewhat more egalitarian distribution of income, it is not necessarily superior in terms of efficiency. They conclude that the overall evidence is too weak to warrant a definitive judgment about a choice of governmental systems.

Furthermore, Tiebout's work (1956) and its recent extensions (for example, Hamilton, 1975) have suggested that local decentralization can lead to an optimal provision of local public services among individuals having different preferences for taxes and services. These studies imply that local decentralization provides a condition in which marketlike solutions can be obtained for the provision of local public goods. Some political scientists have argued that there are also political benefits from local decentralization. According to Dahl (1967), for example, decentralization contributes to American democracy by reducing the burden on the federal government, by allowing greater diversity, by reinforcing the balance of power and authority, and by providing opportunities for citizens to learn about democratic processes.

The conflicting evidence seems to indicate that neither a completely unified system nor a highly fragmented system affords a satisfactory solution to the governance of local areas. Certainly there are benefits associated with an integrated approach to some public sector activities. Nevertheless, these benefits do not seem to warrant a full-scale integration of fragmented local institutions. The wide variety of regional planning arrangements reflects the nature of the quest for an ideal institutional framework.

DEFINITION OF REGIONAL PLANNING

Over the last several decades, regional agencies dealing with a variety of problems of public concern have emerged. The geographical units covered by these agencies vary from groups of small local communities to groups of several states. The term "region" is, therefore, used in a flexible and often ambiguous manner. In the most abstract form, some regional economists define the term as "a spatial subsystem of the national economy" (Siebert, 1969). A definition of this sort serves the purpose of theoretical convenience, but provides little operational meaning. In the broadest sense, a region is a geographical entity which cuts across existing jurisdictional boundaries.

Three approaches have been commonly used to give an operational definition to "region." The first is based on the principle of functional integration. Under this concept, all areas which are functionally tied to the same central node are referred to as a region. The Census definition of a Standard Metropolitan Statistical Area (SMSA) is an approximation of the nodal system of a region. The second approach is the principle of homogeneity. A region is defined by a group of contiguous areas which have similar social and economic characteristics. State Economic Areas (SEAs) established by the Bureau of the Census and Regions defined by the Regional Economics division of the Department of Commerce are examples of this approach. The third approach defines a region for planning-programming purposes. A number of areas can be grouped as a region for the purpose of specific planning goals. For example, the area covered by the Tennessee Valley Authority (TVA) was designated to achieve specific goals such as improvement of navigability, provision for reforestation and proper use of marginal lands, and provision for the national defense. At the metropolitan level, a special purpose or general purpose district can be classified as a region defined for the purposes of planning and programming.

A conventional and probably outdated definition of "planning" refers to activities dealing with physical development such as zoning, land use, park design, and urban renewal. A broader definition refers to public sector efforts to incorporate long-range objectives into the coordination and control of various activities with a look toward the future.[5] Thus, regional planning can be broadly defined as public sector activities encompassing economic, social and physical elements to formulate and implement appropriate public policy in an area covering more than one existing local jurisdiction.[6] For the purpose of inclusiveness and comprehensiveness, the above definiton is used in a broad sense in the following discussion of institutional developments in regional planning.

VARIETIES OF REGIONAL PLANNING INSTITUTIONS

In 1981, a multitude of regional planning agencies exist at various levels of the governmental hierarchy. At the suprastate level, there are such organizations as the TVA, the Delaware River Basin Commission (DRBC), the Appalachian Regional Commission (ARC), the regional economic development commissions under Title V of the Public Works and Economic Development Act of 1965, and the water planning commissions under Title II of the Water Resources Planning Act of 1965.[7] These agencies extend over several states and aim at specific objectives set by the several legislatures. The legacy of suprastate regional planning can be traced to the establishment of the National Resource Planning Board in 1933 which attempted long-range planning and coordination under federal initiative (Beckman, 1960).

At the state level, various departments and commissions are engaged in some type of regional planning. Examples include coastal zone management, land use and housing planning, energy planning, health planning, agricultural land preservation, environmental programs, and flood plain control. These activities usually cover the entire area of the state or a part of the state embracing a number of local jurisdictions. In addition, some states have developed a comprehensive system of regional planning councils.

At the substate level, several approaches to regional planning can be identified. The first is the consolidation of city and county government. In 1977, 73 SMSAs were contained in a single county. For these, city-county consolidation is an attractive option. Following the Baton Rouge model, which came into being in 1949, 62 attempts at city-county consolidation have been documented. Sixteen have been approved by referendum (U.S. Department of Housing and Urban Development, 1980). Examples include Hampton-Elizabeth County, Virginia; Nashville-Davison County, Tennessee; and Jacksonville-Duval County, Florida. While the consolidation approach is very attractive from a theoretical perspective, the traditional weakness of county governments and the existence of strong factional interests raise serious questions about the effectiveness of this approach. Thus, a second approach has been to strengthen existing urban counties by expanding the service responsibility of county governments and by increasing their tax-raising abilities. Los Angeles County, well known for the Lakewood Plan (Cion, 1971), exemplifies the urban county approach.

A third type of substate regional planning is a system of two-tier government. This approach was promoted by the Committee for Economic Development (CED) in 1970. The logic of this approach is that American cities have two different needs: one for jurisdictions large enough to cope with problems that pervade entire regions and the other for jurisdictions small enough to allow grass roots participation. The two best known examples of two-tier government in North America are Miami and Toronto.

The fourth approach is the creation of a regional government. In 1981, there are only two metropolitan regional governments in the United States: Portland, established by the electorate, and Minneapolis-St. Paul, established by the state legislature. A regional government is an independent legal entity with its own financial resources. It is governed by a board representing the entire region, and it serves multiple purposes. The regional government approach is by far the most comprehensive and operates at the highest level of integration.

The fifth and most popular approach is the Council of Governments (COG). The number of COGs increased from 23 in 1950 to 670 in 1980 (U.S. Department of Housing and Urban Development, 1980). This phenomenal growth is due at least partially to federal encouragement. In order to coordinate the planning activities of the various localities within a metropolitan area, the federal government has fostered such instruments as 701 Comprehensive Planning, 208 Water Quality Planning, 175 Air Quality Planning, Coastal Zone Management, Solid Waste Management, Health Systems Agencies, and the A-95 Review Process. Another reason for the popularity of COGs can be found in their structure and function. Unlike metropolitan governments, Councils of Governments are usually formed by voluntary agreements between localities and are governed by a board of local representatives. Their functions are limited to information exchange, cooperation, coordination, technical assistance, and provision of some services. COGs are therefore much easier to establish. Examples of COGs are the Miami Valley Regional Planning Commission, the Association of Bay Area Governments, and the Metropolitan Washington Council of Governments.

A sixth approach to substate regional planning takes the form of special-purpose districts. Some examples of this method are the Bay Area Rapid Transit District (BART) in San Francisco, the Port Authority of New York and New Jersey, and the Chicago Sanitary District. These agencies provide specific services to an entire region.

Table 2 shows the various approaches to regional planning in the United States classified by the level of government and by the form of the regional planning agency. According to a survey by the 1977 Census of Government, 3,044 of the 3,070 counties in the United States are served by at least one regional organization: 994 of these counties are served by three agencies, 506 of them by four agencies, and 171 of them by five or more agencies. These data reflect a tremendous growth in the number and extent of regional planning activities as well as the variety of styles in institutional arrangements.

SCOPE AND PLAN OF THE VOLUME

The vulnerability of regional planning agencies as political and economic institutions lies in their multijurisdictional nature and in the political divergency of their constituencies. Successful operation of these agencies depends heavily on the political and financial participation of local jurisdictions as well as on federal and state support. The aftermath of Proposition 13 proffers some evidence of how financial constraints originating from local institutions affect regional planning activities.[8] The drastic cutback in federal support for regional planning, which was proposed by the Reagan Administration and ratified by the Congress, will no doubt force most regional planning agencies to undertake substantial institutional changes. In addition to reduced financial resources, changes in regulatory processes related to regional planning will further

TABLE 2

CLASSIFICATION OF REGIONAL PLANNING ACTIVITIES

Level	Type	Examples
Suprastate	Suprastate Regional Planning	TVA, DRBC, ARC Title V Commissions Title II Commissions
State	Statewide Regional Planning	State Regional Councils State Land Use Planning State Coastal Zone Management
Substate	City-County Consolidation	Baton Rouge, Louisiana Jacksonville, Florida Newport, Virginia Nashville, Tennessee
	Urban County	Los Angeles County, California Dade County, Florida
	Two-Tier Gov't	Miami, Florida Toronto, Canada
	Metropolitan Gov't	Minneapolis-St. Paul, Minnesota Portland, Oregon
	Council of Gov'ts	Miami Valley Reg'l Planning Comm'n Metropolitan Washington COG Association of Bay Area Gov'ts Atlanta Regional Commission
	Special-Purpose Districts	BART Port Authority of N.Y. and N.J. Chicago Sanitary District

increase the pressure on regional planning agencies to alter and restructure their operations.

Faced with these pressures, regional planning agencies may consider several alternatives. They may continue their current activities by obtaining financial support from other sources, such as the state or the private sector. They may reduce their activities and adjust their functions to respond to the reduction in financial resources. As a hybrid of the above two alternatives, they may attempt to reorganize their functions and activities and simultaneously increase their financial support from other sources. Finally, regional planning agencies may be completely dismantled.

The first alternative seems viable only for those agencies not highly dependent on federal support. Since state and private contributions are clearly limited, agencies with a high level of financial dependency on federal support may have to reduce substantially their activities. Realistically, many regional planning agencies are likely to take the second or third alternative. The scope of reduction in their activities and the nature of change in their functions will depend on the local political situation as well as on the degree of financial cutback. It is quite possible that eventually some agencies will be dissolved.

Some critics envision the current policy change as an opportunity to eliminate regional planning agencies for good. However, this last option should be considered only after a careful evaluation of long-run costs and benefits. Given the political decentralization and territorial fragmentation firmly grounded in the political and social values of the country, any endeavor to bring the ideal of regional planning to reality incurs considerable political and other tangible and intangible costs. Dismantling regional planning agencies may waste valuable political and economic resources invested in past decades by government and private groups in institutional developments. Sensible reform and reorganization of regional planning institutions would require a thorough evaluation of the options and a careful consideration of the specific political, social, and economic conditions in which they operate.

This volume focuses on the issues facing regional planning at the state and substate levels. Although it does not pretend to cover all the issues of regional planning at these levels, it presents a cross-section of problems and concerns, and it offers a set of representative functional issues and agency cases from which some meaningful generalizations can be drawn. The most critical issue debated and discussed throughout the volume is the appropriate role of regional planning given the particular economic and political environment of the country. Some of the papers examine the role of regional planning and review its contribution in a broad context. Others evaluate in more detail the impact of the current shift in federal policies and local attitudes on regional planning.

Part Two of the volume deals with conceptual issues. William Cassella presents an historical overview and a political account of the development of regional planning in the United States (Chapter 2). Bruce McDowell examines the influence of the federal government on the development of regional planning activities and the current Administration's move to withdraw federal support for regional planning (Chapter 3).

Part Three is concerned with functional issues in regional planning. Patrick Holland discusses the political and institutional conflicts between municipalities and the role of the federal government in regional planning for solid waste disposal (Chapter 4). Alden McClellan and Brian Boxer examine the development of coastal zone management as a regional issue and analyze the impact of federal policies (Chapter 5). Roger Vaughan argues that planning in the past has made little contribution to economic development and proposes a model for economic development planning (Chapter 6). Jack Boyd diagnoses the nature of regional health planning and presents his concern for the future of regional health agencies (Chapter 7). Richard Page looks at the issue of transportation finance and describes the political and institutional problems experienced by some localities (Chapter 8).

Part Four presents four case studies of regional planning agencies. Ted Kolderie examines the reasons for the success of the Twin Cities' Metropolitan Council (Chapter 9). Ingrid Reed discusses the problems faced by the Tri-State Regional Planning Commission and examines its future role (Chapter 10). Denton Kent describes the experience of the most revolutionary experiment in regional planning—the Portland METRO (Chapter 11). Nancy Stroud presents an analysis of the state's role in regional planning, using Florida as a case study (Chapter 12).

Finally, Charles Warren summarizes the main themes, issues, agreements, and disagreements presented by the papers and outlines his views about the future of regional planning (Chapter 13).

PART TWO

Conceptual Issues

2. Regional Planning and Governance: History and Politics

William N. Cassella, Jr.

EARLY APPROACHES

> Perhaps it is not too much to expect that the near future may
> bring to the metropolitan district(s) . . . a form which shall
> preserve to the several cities and towns as they now exist the
> full control over their local affairs and give to a central rep-
> resentative council full control over . . . metropolitan mat-
> ters.

Neither the near nor the distant future saw the realization of these
great expectations expressed at the National Municipal League's
annual conference in 1909 (National Municipal League, 1909, p.
214).

Planning and governance in the metropolitan regions of America
has taken myriad forms never so neat as that envisioned by some
early Twentieth Century reformers. Indeed, the vision conceived
in their minds ignored the host of political, economic, social, and
technical realities which were already shaping the future of every

urban region. Early in the century, reordering government in metropolitan areas took its place along side other reforms promoted by good government leagues, municipal research bureaus, and some political scientists. But unlike scientific management, city planning, executive reorganization, and even the short ballot, which could be presented in definitive model packages, it was soon apparent that there was no single solution for the problems of regional governance.

In 1922, Chester C. Maxey, then on the faculty of Cleveland's Western Reserve University, in the first systematic round-up of experience in metropolitan reorganization, talked of how the metropolis faced the handicap of political disintegration, the "struggle for civic achievement amid the conflicts, dissensions, and divergencies of its several political jurisdictions . . . political dismemberment of a metropolitan community." He recognized that in no two communities are conditions precisely the same, yet in all, the fundamental difficulty is political disunity (Maxey, 1922, p. 229).

In 1930, a special committee of the National Municipal League completed the first comprehensive study of the government of metropolitan areas and stated that "it had no panacea or formula to be applied indiscriminately to all regions." The committee spoke with approval of the "regional planning movement which ignores old municipal boundary lines as frequently being arbitrary and obsolete. But to be of value plans must be executed. The loose clusters of municipal units . . . are impotent to give reality to the vision of planners." The committee perceived that this would be a challenge to political scientists and planners, that "the task confronting our urban areas is one of political reconstruction calling for high statesmanship and sound political wisdom" (National Municipal League, 1930, p. 4).

Ten years later, Thomas H. Reed, whose influence as a consultant in governmental reorganization was widespread in achieving improved management structures, reported that "progress in solving the problems which arise from the maladjustment of the areas of local government to the needs of metropolitan communities has been insignificant" (Reed, 1941, p. 400). But he predicted that "the time will come . . . when our anachronistic and unwieldly system of local government will quietly collapse and a more rational system emerge." Yet another decade later he was forced to observe, "Many better and wiser city planners and political scientists than myself have poured out millions of words by tongue, pen, and typewriter on the same theme, but frankness requires me to say so far we have accomplished little more than a world's record for words used in proportion to cures effected." Nevertheless, again as he described the crippling disease he called suburbanitis, he expressed confidence that "as we have solved so many other problems of organization and procedure in local government, in spite of the intense opposition of politicians and deadening pessimism of the public we shall in good time—not too far off—conquer 'suburbanitis'" (Reed, 1950, p. 542).

Over the next 30 years, the flow of words has continued relentlessly. The metropolitan problem became part of the urban crisis of the 1960 s and involved much more than political disunity and governmental fragmentation. The central city-suburban conflict was laced with elements of racial discord and discrimination, blight in all forms, disastrous disparities between needs and resources, dogmatic functional feudalism, and an infinite number of political turf problems, both imagined and real. Urban America was spread city, and its governmental framework and fiscal structure were becoming more rather than less complex.

INSTITUTIONAL DEVELOPMENT

Concern for meeting urban needs expressed itself in more than words because an affluent society put its money where its mouth was. Expenditures increased dramatically with all manner of urban programs initially financed largely by federal dollars. These new programs in turn gave birth to several generations of studies and reports and an "intergovernmentalizing" of just about every public service. There were national studies, state studies, metropolitan studies, and local studies. Most were problem-oriented, some were called plans, some proposed new governmental structures, some sought to strengthen existing units, and some were parts of new interlevel, interjurisdictional initiatives; almost all said that we need to have better coordination of policy and capital planning among units and levels. We heard about massive cooperation efforts such as UMJOs (Umbrella Multi-Jurisdiction Organizations). There were new specialized regional agencies, including CAMPS (Cooperative Area Manpower Planning Systems), EDDs (Economic Development Districts), RTPAs (Regional Transportation Planning Agencies), and CHPA s (Comprehensive Health Planning Agencies), all of which came after 1950. Local government was inundated with the new alphabet soup of federally inspired activity. It made the New Deal alphabet brew look thin. During the 1950s, academic pioneers like Paul Studenski and Victor Jones were joined by a procession of scholars. Some were part of the new urban studies programs in the universities. Some were looking at the public finance implications of government in metropolitan areas. Others were urban planners focusing on regional matters. There was the new discipline of regional science.

For all of us with a concern for the government of metropolitan areas, 1950 was the watershed. The terrain was 168 Standard Metropolitan Areas with 16,210 units of local government. Many of us had confidence that in the post-World War II era, with adequate research and diligent political effort, local government could be reshaped to deal more effectively with the real or regional city. We soon found that citizens generally did not share our concern or reform conviction. Indeed, many were frightened by the prospect of disturbing well-established jurisdictional patterns and political behavior habits. Those in power more often than not were lined up against even relatively modest redesigns in structure. The vocal radical right opposition denounced every metropolitan reform as a METRO and part of a communist plot. Their evidence included the fact that the Moscow subway is called the METRO.

There were many important landmarks in the 1950s, events which moved the problem of metropolitan government out of the special realm of academe and the good government groups. The pre-World War II period had seen its share of defeats of metropolitan reorganization. Therefore, the first significant postwar success in Baton Rouge in the late 1940s received much attention in 1950. That year Atlanta adopted its "plan for improvement," completely realigning relationships between the City of Atlanta and Fulton County. In 1953, the Ontario parliament approved the federated Municipality of Metropolitan Toronto. Congress included in the Housing Act of 1954 direct federal assistance to metropolitan and regional planning agencies which sparked new interest in regional planning. The National Municipal League responded by preparing the *Model State and Regional Planning Law* (1954).

In 1955, the Commission on Intergovernmental Relations, the so-called Kestnbaum Commission, reported that metropolitan areas . . . are the most important focal points of intergovernmental relations . . . The National Government has an obligation to facilitate State action with respect to metropolitan problems. It should begin by analysing the impact of its activities on metropolitan areas and by working with the States for better coordination of National and State policies and programs in such areas (U.S. Commission on Intergovernmental Relations, 1955, p.51).

The same year, the National Governors' Conference directed the Council of State Governments to study the problem of government in metropolitan areas. The council's report stressed the responsibilities "for the states to assume in working cooperatively with local governments . . . toward an adequate solution of the metropolitan problem" (Council of State Governments, 1955).

The next year at the invitation of Nelson Rockefeller, chairman of the Government Affairs Foundation, 250 persons from 28 states, the District of Columbia, and two Canadian provinces met for three days in East Lansing, Michigan for the first National Conference on Metropolitan Area Problems. This meeting was called "to initiate a broadly representative exchange of ideas concerning: 1) the cause and nature of the difficulties facing our urban areas, particularly those related to governmental problems; 2) alternative routes to 'solutions'; 3) types of further knowledge and understanding required for progress; and 4) development of methods of sound, effective action." The conference was a remarkable mix of political, business, labor, civic, academic, and media people. Mayor Daley of Chicago, Governor Mennen Williams of Michigan, as well as Nelson Rockefeller, were among the speakers. The conference was a milestone in stressing cooperation among governmental, civic, and professional organizations as they addressed the problems of metropolitan areas. It launched a unique consortium of these organizations as the Continuing Conference on Metropolitan Area Problems which proved a valuable network for the balance of the decade. However, like so many laudable efforts launched by philanthropic generosity, when the angel flew off to other undertakings, in this case the governorship of New York, the momentum could not be sustained. Nevertheless, a successor operation sponsored by the Institute of Public Administration and the State University of New York at Albany continued as a most useful resource through 1970.

Another contribution of the Rockefeller-sponsored program was the development of a compendium of metropolitan surveys and an annotated bibliography, which reached monumental proportions. The initial volume published in 1956 contained 5,120 entries. Four supplementary volumes added 15,454 more references to the literature of the 1950s and 1960s. These document the flood stage in the torrent of words, which rose even higher during the 1970s.

The words told many stories and proved or disproved many hypotheses. In the 1950s and 1960s unprecedented attention was given to the metropolis from literally every point of view. The number of official reports and unofficial studies was tremendous. The advent of the computer permitted many of these to be quantified as never before.

Also in 1959, a remarkable meeting, the first Urban County Congress, was held in Washington, D.C. This event celebrated a drastic change in the image of county government and made a strong statement for its role as a major partner in the planning and governance of metropolitan areas. It signaled that at least some counties had moved out of the "dark continent" as they had been characterized earlier in the century. The vice president of the United States and several U.S. senators were in attendance, as were an impressive array of county officials who had their eyes on urban matters. The new importance of counties was emphasized by giving particular attention to the adoption of the new Miami Dade County metropolitan charter and a number of other examples of county reform.

In a very dramatic way, this congress focused on the strength and diversity of local political traditions, on the central political reality of regional governance and of regional planning as well. In those states where states' rights lingered longest as desideratum, less emphasis was placed on home rule. There, centralization at the state and county levels had wide acceptance. Paradoxically, in those states where there was less opposition to national government intervention, the home rule and town meeting tradition was extremely strong. Even county government was thought of as big government. Perhaps our optimism was fed by the fact that this tradition seemed to be in ferment in the 1950s. The one-room school district had succumbed to consolidation. Counties were taking on new functions, primarily those which cities were eager to release, such as health and welfare. But it was clear that very little in the way of institution rebuilding was going to occur without the support of a substantial part of established political leadership.

A most significant initiative at the end of the 1950s was the establishment of the Advisory Commission on Intergovernmental Relations (ACIR). Its studies and reports have made a major contribution to accumulated knowledge on metropolitan governance. The ACIR has provided a wealth of analysis on fiscal disparities within and between regions, a vast substate regionalism study, and its more recent review in *Regionalism Revisited: Recent Areawide and Local Responses* (ACIR, 1977). The ACIR has fostered a regionalism which is multifunctional and multijurisdictional for planning and coordination purposes.

During the 1950s, there seemed to be a new willingness on the part of political leaders to permit and even encourage the study of regional problems as long as they were, in some way, participants. From 1950 to 1960, more studies were initiated than in the three previous decades. In this climate, a number of the studies led to proposals which came to public referendum. Reformers were somewhat disillusioned by the results. The ACIR surveyed 18 referenda of which only eight resulted in voter approval of change (ACIR, 1962). The proposals covered a considerable variety of approaches to metropolitan reorganization ranging from city-county consolidation to internal restructuring of counties. The ACIR study cited many of the political issues encountered such as the status of individual elected officers, the constituencies of members of elected bodies, and the attachments to existing units, notably by public employees.

Significantly, the politics of reorganization show not only opposition from the status quo, but also from those who want to take another approach. Typically, for example, consolidationists reject more modest compromise solutions. Also, there is the persistent problem of any new arrangement costing more. However, the most important problem is public apathy and disinterest. In the 18 referenda studies by the ACIR, only one in four eligible voters bothered to vote, and it is well known that it is easier to get out the vote against than the vote for. "If you don't know, then vote NO." Thus reform in metropolitan governance is particularly difficult when there are constitutional or statutory requirements for referenda. A legitimate question is whether legislative solutions without referenda, considering the low voter turnout, may actually be a more accurate reflection of the public interest.

Whether it is to occur by legislation or referenda, any successful approach to an improvement of regional governance and planning will not take place unless community leaders acquire a more adequate understanding of their region and its problems. A note-worthy national effort to that end was undertaken by the Committee for Economic Development (CED). Its attention to metropolis began in the late 1950s and has resulted in three major policy statements which take their place alongside CED's influential position on economic issues: *Guiding Metropolitan Growth* (CED, 1960), *Modernizing Local Government* (CED, 1966), and *Reshaping Government in Metropolitan Areas* (CED, 1970).

In the case of New York, the largest metropolitan region in the country, a continuing effort to provide policy guidance for regional leaders has been conducted by the Regional Plan Association (RPA). For the RPA, the 1950s was the beginning of a new era with its massive studies projecting what the region would look like in 1985 if trends continued, and a decade-long process of research, deliberation, and community dialogue which led to the Second Regional Plan. To implement the Plan, RPA has provided guidance for intervention which can modify trends and promote sound development and redevelopment.

Another development of the 1950s was the first stage of a strategy which has far-reaching implications for regional governance. It was the Council of Governments (COG) movement. A report to the Ford Foundation called "the most striking and probably the most important institutional development in metropolis . . . the proliferation of councils of governments" (Danielson, Hershey, and Bayne, 1977, p.73). Bringing together the major elected local officials of a region, this movement was a direct response to the political reality of a well-established pattern of local government. If change was to come, these officials were to be a part of the change. There seemed to be a willingness to make some adjustments if on a voluntary basis. The establishment of the Inter-County Supervisors Committee in the Detroit area in 1956 was followed by a train of others, many stimulated by the influx of federal dollars.

Some participants and observers in this development saw it as a mixed blessing. It was a good vehicle to increase regional consciousness, to develop mutual understanding of common problems, and to provide a channel of interunit communication and perhaps some program coordination. Yet it was lacking because COG participation was a secondary concern to all the representatives of local government; they wore two hats: one local and one regional. Indeed, some called it institutionalized parochialism. Another concern was the constant changing cast of characters because of local election calendars. While giving the COG movement a positive assessment, the ACIR did note the special problem of the "limited interest, power, and time of participants" (ACIR, 1966). COGs have understandably found it more comfortable to deal with the less controversial aspects of growth and development, transportation and parks, rather than such issues as low-income housing needs, central city decay, and the location of waste disposal facilities.

Although the COG movement began as a voluntary association of officials and has continued to maintain that essential quality, it was the availability of federal funds which provided the major stimulus for the striking increase in the number of COGs, and with federal funds comes official status—a far cry from the informality of the earlier voluntary associations. COG staffs have been in the main highly competent professionals who, as full time public agency heads, have sometimes tended to overshadow the part-time representatives of local government. The most effective COG operations have been those in which the local government representatives themselves utilized the resources of their own staffs to strengthen their participation.

Unquestionably, the COG effort would have achieved little more than symbolic results if federal funds had not been available to support some of its research and planning programs and if the definition of "regional councils" had been restricted to groups composed entirely of elected local officials. The movement was enriched when COGs joined with the appointed regional planning bodies in the National Association of Regional Councils. As noted earlier, a major event during the 1950s' saga of regional planning was the 1954 Housing Act's provision of financial assistance for metropolitan planning agencies, so-called 701 assistance. Until then, the number of official multijurisdictional planning commissions was minimal. County planning boards were filling that role in single county metropolitan areas. However, even with a modest federal appropriation, the number of agencies multiplied; by 1960 they were found in nearly one-half of the metropolitan areas. The ACIR has documented the story of how federal intervention was responsible for the spread of the regional council phenomenon, how in the course of a very few years, both appointed regional planning commissions and councils of elected officials have almost literally covered the nation, how they assumed the clearinghouse function for federal grants, and how in some cases they were forerunners of other mechanisms for regional governance (ACIR, 1973, p. 49f).

The regional council is now appearing in a variety of models, some very different from the COGs of the 1950s, which blossomed in the 1960s and 1970s. Unquestionably, it was a vehicle which stimulated regional planning and some coordination. A very useful purpose served by the COGs and the older regional planning commissions was as the transition phase towards a more sophisticated concept of regional planning and governance. Another valuable contribution of the regional councils has been their "generalist" character in a scene increasingly characterized by functional feudalism or "vertical functional autocracy," as some call it. A great deal of planning at the regional level has been in a function-by-function manner by special districts. This sort of fragmentation can be the quintessence of bureaucratic isolation.

FUTURE OF REGIONAL PLANNING

It is imperative to stress that regional planning will have little significance if it is considered only as an intellectual or professional exercise or is isolated from the real world of politics. To be meaningful, it must be considered as part of governance, and with the realization that urban regions in American federalism will always be governed by a maze of political units. They will never be converted into neat and orderly entities by adjusting boundary lines, consolidating units, and building new structures just to eliminate duplication and achieve economies of scale, nor will there ever be clearly differentiated roles which will eliminate interunit, interlevel, and interfunctional controversy. Some of this controversy is the yeast of a free system, but deliberation need not be the confrontation of absolute positions. Some means for assuring representative expression of the contending interests is a constant institutional goal. Almost every conceivable approach has been tried somewhere in the last century, and knowledge of these efforts helps prevent us from reinventing the wheel, but this should not dissuade us from trying new experiments, knowing that none will be the universal, absolute solution to regional governance. Regional planning mechanisms can be developed in the context of existing structures, and even these are susceptible to some retooling.

This is a particularly auspicious time to focus on adjustments in the intergovernmental fabric because some reordering of responsibilities is clearly underway. Whether it is called new federalism or partnership, there is a ferment which presages change. Depending on one's point of view, the change may be for the better or for the worse, but change there will be. Over the years, the role of the federal government expanded, and now it is beginning to contract. It is evident that although states have given a very inconsistent performance, they have assumed a more positive and creative posture. They seem to have a greater awareness that better coordination of their own programs in urban regions is essential. Many state efforts have been directed to this end and to improve the capacity of local government. Special state commissions and legislative committees have reported on such issues as regional and community development, and structural reforms, among others.

Almost certainly, the role of states in regional governance will increase. It has been more than ten years since the American Assembly concluded that states were central urban actors (Campbell, 1970). Like it or not, states are now on stage and regional concerns must be part of their legislative repertoire. Involving elected local officials in regional planning and governance is an accepted fact; witness the COG movement. In some of the COG organizations with the most constructive performance, state legislators have been key participants. Regional governance will increasingly assign important roles to state legislative leaders working in conjunction with other elected officials, both state and local. Also of growing importance are state community affairs agencies. Their national organization, the Council of State Community Affairs Agencies (COSCAA), can play a strategic role in the evolution of state-local relationships in a new federalism.

As we consider the future of regional planning, we must recognize that literally all levels of government are somehow involved, and also that many major decisions of regional import will be made in the private sector. It is necessary to understand the potential of both unofficial regional planning and the planning and operations of official agencies.

Whenever we combine "regional" and "planning," there will be debate as to its process and substance. A 1964 study, conducted by the Joint Center for Urban Studies, Massachusetts Institute of Technology and Harvard University, concluded "that now is the time to move ahead in encouraging the growth of the existing embryonic system into a more permanent and responsive structure of metropolitan planning" (U.S. Senate Subcommittee on

Intergovernmental Relations, 1964). Nearly two decades later, encouragement is still needed, but we are more keenly aware of the necessity of relating planning to implementation.

The purpose of this paper has been to place approaches to regional planning in historical and political perspective. It could not, in this brief compass, cover the complete saga of regional planning and governance during the last several decades. The serious analyst must cover the vast field of how regions fit into a federal system which itself is in transition. Perhaps there will be a much greater role for the regional agency as a substate instrument if states assume greater discretion. It is possible that regions are a midpoint at which state and local considerations can be better served than by the traditional levels.

It is appropriate and still timely to quote the Joint Center report.

> Although the federal system is conceptually divisible into several layers of government, historically all levels have cooperated in dealing with problems affecting the governed. This traditional sharing of functions is especially important with respect to programs affecting metropolitan development . . . Federal legislation encouraging metropolitan planning is premised upon and respects the separate existence of local units of government; it is in no way a preface to metropolitan supergovernment . . . In the final analysis the course of metropolitan planning and cooperation is and must continue to be governed by the cumulative orientations of the governments at the state and local levels and the public at large (U.S. Senate Subcommittee on Intergovernmental Relations, 1964, p. 38, 117-19).

3. The Federal Role in Regional Planning: Past and Present

Bruce D. McDowell

INTRODUCTION

This paper tells two very different stories.[1] The first tells how a number of federal initiatives, taken over a period of two decades, slowly but steadily built a network of regional planning organizations throughout the nation. The second is the story of federal support for these organizations being withdrawn almost completely within a period of one year.

STORY ONE: FEDERAL INITIATIVES

The federal government first became conscious of areawide problems in metropolitan areas during World War I while overseeing the construction of war housing. It became apparent in this process that suburban areas were ill prepared to accommodate new growth (Hand, McDowell, and So, forthcoming, Chapter 2).

As metropolitan planning organizations were established in a number of major urban areas during the 1920s, mostly by local

29

initiatives, the federal government's recognition of interjurisdictional needs began to crystallize. In 1929, Herbert Hoover appointed the President's Research Committee on Social Trends. That committee recommended establishment of a nationwide network of planning efforts stretching from the national level to the local level. The recommendation was supported in a number of ways by President Roosevelt's National Planning Board, later to become the National Resources Planning Board. Concerning the regional level, the Board supported a seven-county interstate metropolitan planning effort in the St. Louis area, as a model for other metropolitan efforts throughout the nation, and urged Congress to authorize interstate compacts for metropolitan planning in the nation's 22 interstate metropolitan areas.[2] A 1937 report by one of the Board's committees recommended metropolitan and other planning efforts throughout the nation.

During the 1950s, federal grants became available directly to metropolitan planning commissions through the Housing and Home Finance Agency, predecessor to the Department of Housing and Urban Development, and a substantial amount of federal highway planning money given to the states found its way into major urban area transportation studies. By 1960, approximately two-thirds of the nation's existing 212 metropolitan areas were engaged in some type of areawide planning. The typical form of organization during this whole period was the independently appointed planning commission composed of "blue ribbon" private citizens, although some were *ad hoc* transportation study committees made up largely of state and local transportation agency representatives.

Up to this point, federal and state initiatives were really quite mild. While the federal government had recommended metropolitan planning, and provided some funds for it in those areas which took initiatives to request grants, the critical factor remained local initiative. There were no federal requirements for metropolitan planning and the state role was largely limited to enacting enabling legislation which could become effective only with local initiative and to using some federal highway planning funds in urban areas having major transportation problems. The low-key approach changed dramatically in the 1960s and 1970s, shifting from passive to active.

Early in the 1960s, the federal aid programs for highways, mass transit, and open space began requiring metropolitan planning as a condition for obtaining federal action grants in those fields. Then, in 1965, the Department of Housing and Urban Development's (HUD) Sec. 701 Comprehensive Planning funds were made available to areawide organizations of locally elected officials, commonly referred to as Councils of Government. The Department of Commerce's new economic development program began making funds available for the support of multicounty economic development districts. Section 204 of the Housing Act of 1966 contained a requirement that all applications for federal aid in a wide variety of community development projects in metropolitan areas be reviewed and commented upon by the metropolitan planning organization in affected areas. Following these breakthroughs, a large number of regional planning requirements and assistance programs were enacted. These concentrated on metropolitan areas throughout the 1960s but encompassed regions as well during the 1970s. By 1979, some 39 distinct federal programs were financially supporting or requiring regional planning (Stam and Reid, 1980), and 99 percent of all counties, or county areas in those states without active county governments, were encompassed within the jurisdiction of substate regional planning organizations (Bureau of the Census, 1978). The array of federal aids encompassed the fields of rural development, community and economic development, environmental protection, transportation, health and social services, protective services, and general purposes. Also, a federal push to involve the states encouraged 44 states to establish statewide systems of substate districts (Advisory Commission on Intergovernmental Relations, 1973; forthcoming).

The federal initiatives of the last two decades not only spread substate regionalism nationwide, but transformed the "blue ribbon" private citizen regional planning commissions into Councils of Governments. They also greatly expanded the scope of regional work programs and the size of staffs, and changed small budgets dependent primarily on local contributions into large budgets heavily dependent on federal funding. In addition, a number of federal programs established networks of special purpose regional organizations in the same regions served by the general purpose planning commissions or councils of government. Chief among the special purpose bodies are health systems agencies, areawide or countywide community action agencies, area agencies on the aging, manpower planning councils, criminal justice planning organizations, and resource conservation and development councils. In a few cases, functions like urban transportation planning and water quality planning also are carried out by special purpose areawide organizations instead of by general purpose ones. While the general purpose regional councils were about 76 percent dependent on federal funding in 1977, the special purpose organizations derived about 92 percent of their funds from federal grants (Bureau of the Census, 1978).

The nation's large multistate economic development commissions frequently provided significant support for substate regions in the 1970s (Hand, McDowell, and So, forthcoming). The Appalachian Regional Commission was in the forefront of this activity, devising a planning system which relied heavily upon aggregating well-developed substate regional plans into state plans, which in turn provided the oasis for the Appalachian regional plan. By 1979, five of the ten Title V multistate economic development commissions also supported substate regional planning.

As the 1970s ended, the nation was virtually covered with both substate and multistate regional planning organizations having active planning programs. The vitality of these programs and their geographic extent had been greatly enhanced by numerous federal initiatives (Hand, McDowell, and So, forthcoming, Chapter 2).

STORY TWO: FEDERAL WITHDRAWAL

On February 18, 1981, President Reagan proposed his new budget in a document entitled *America's New Beginning: A Program for Economic Recovery.* He proposed to eliminate most of the federal supports for substate and multistate regional planning, to fold certain other federal programs into new block grants, and to cut the amount of funding for still others.

1. For elimination, the President nominated: HUD's Section 701 Comprehensive Planning grants, the Economic Development Administration's (EDA) grants for the support of economic development districts, the Environmental Protection Agency's (EPA) Section 208 water quality planning program, Agriculture's rural development program, the Appalachian Regional Commission's grants for the support of local development districts (as well as all its other funding, except highways), support for health systems agencies, grants for community action agencies, regional planning (and all other) funds under the coastal zone management program, and all support for the Title V commissions

including their support for substate regionalism. Already being phased out by the Carter Administration was the criminal justice planning program of the Law Enforcement Assistance Administration (LEAA).

2. The health and human services block grants proposed in the President's Fiscal 1982 budget carried the potential for consolidating certain programs such as the emergency medical program and community mental health centers, which had been sources of support for substate regionalism in some areas. Such consolidation would leave the role of regional organizations unclear.

3. Funding for every other program supporting regional planning and related activities was subject to budget cuts.

4. The urban and secondary highway systems were to be phased out within two years, while operating subsidies for transit were to be eliminated in Fiscal 1982. At the same time, the capital expenditure programs for highways and transit facilities were proposed to shift over to maintenance and the purchase of buses, and away from new construction. These changes called into question the need for the traditional urban transportation planning process and the metropolitan planning organizations (MPOs).

Although Congress made a number of changes in block grant formats and provided somewhat more transitional funding than Reagan proposed, most of the President's proposals with respect to substate regionalism have been enacted. Except for some urban transportation planning and areawide aging funds and some transition funding from HUD, EDA, and the Department of Health and Human Services (HHS), the federal government has withdrawn its financial support from the substate regional movement.

Deregulation, one of the campaign promises of President Reagan, has been given high priority within the Administration. The air quality program is being reevaluated, while the urban transportation planning regulations are being rethought with the idea of reducing the number of social goals which they try to promote, such as energy conservation, air quality improvement, and services to the handicapped. In addition, the A-95 project notification and review process adminstered by the U.S. Office of Management and Budget (OMB) through about 550 state and areawide clearinghouses, most of which are substate regional councils, was added to the Vice President's list of regulations targeted for modification or elimination. Indeed, total elimination and an option which would place the existence and functions of A-95 clearinghouses entirely at the discretion of the states already are working their way up the chain of command at OMB.

In proposing to eliminate HUD's Section 701 comprehensive planning assistance program, the President noted that "The primary intent of this program—to develop sub-national planning capabilities—has been realized." He went on to argue that the type of planning done with these funds is that for which the subnational units of government have responsibility; they should, therefore, provide the funding for it.

The Administration's rationale for block grants is much the same as for phasing out HUD's planning grants. The fields in which the blocks have been proposed are those in which the Administration believes that other levels of government hold responsibility. At least for now, Congress seems to have accepted this rationale. Accountability for planning and administering the new block grants is largely left to the state and local electorates rather than to federal administrators. It is also proposed that block grants be phased out completely within a few years as tax resources are returned to the state and local levels.

Despite the fact that the substate regions have worked diligently to help promote nationally legislated goals for equal housing opportunity, economic opportunity, improved air quality, improved water quality, energy conservation, preparations for energy emergencies, federal interagency project coordination, and other purposes, the federal government has very largely withdrawn its support from these organizations. President Reagan has pledged further efforts at cutting the budget, expanding the coverage of block grants, and wiping out still more federal regulations. There appears little chance that federal help for regional organizations will revive in the foreseeable future.

SPECULATIONS ON THE FUTURE

Where does all of this leave the regional organizations? The nation's Title V multistate economic development commissions and Title II river basin commissions closed down on September 30, 1981. The Appalachian Regional Commission is being phased out in Fiscal 1982. A recent survey by the National Association of

Regional Councils indicates that perhaps 10 percent of the substate regional bodies will go out of business in 1982. Another 50 percent of these regional councils may experience budget cuts of as much as 60 percent during this period. The picture is not a pretty one.

However, it should be remembered that most of the original metropolitan planning commissions established in the 1920s and 1930s resulted from local initiatives, not federal or state ones. Two-thirds of all metropolitan areas had regional planning organizations before federal requirements came along. There are needs for areawide planning that are obvious and compelling. In addition, more regional councils frequently are involved in areawide programs than the number required by federal rules and regulations (Advisory Commission on Intergovernmental Relations, forthcoming). Such programs include air and water quality, social services, community action, rural development, health systems, solid wastes, and rural transportation.

The past two decades have institutionalized areawide planning and demonstrated the many ways in which regional planning organizations can be useful. State laws in every state except Delaware and Hawaii provide for the establishment of regional planning organizations, and every state has some regional planning activity within it. Most states have policies and procedures which promote and take advantage of the benefits from regional planning. About half of the states support their regions financially, although this support is very small in all but six states. The average metropolitan planning budget is about $1 million, and it would still have about $250,000 left after subtracting all federal funds. In nonmetropolitan areas, the average budget would shrink from $350,000 to $88,000 with complete federal withdrawal. Remaining funds would be sufficient to maintain an organization. Thus, there is reason to believe that the state and local governments can be expected to provide for the continuation of some regional planning.

Nevertheless, present times will be difficult for state and local governments as well as for regional organizations. A majority of the federal budget cuts are being made in aid to state and local governments at the same time that these governments are feeling the press of constitutional limitations on their own revenue-raising capabilities. The states and localities are having to cut back their own operations at the very time that regions would hope to make up at least part of the decrease in their federal revenues from the state and local coffers. The conclusion must be, therefore, that most federal budget cuts felt by the regional bodies will be real ones.

Staff layoffs, some of very substantial proportions, already have begun in most regional councils. The special purpose regional planning organizations sponsored by federal programs are likely to disappear in much larger numbers than the general purpose regional councils. This is because they have so few dollars, only eight percent, from other sources. This provides an opportunity for some of the essential purposes of these special organizations to be picked up by the general purpose ones.

The quality and scope of planning work done by regional councils almost certainly will deteriorate as funding and federal requirements wither. Few states have planning requirements to take the place of the federal ones which are being withdrawn. Even the project notification and review process, known as A-95 at the federal level, has been legislated infrequently at the state level. States also lack the incentive to require areawide planning in interstate metropolitan areas.

It is most likely that requests for fuller state support for regions, to compensate for federal withdrawal, will be responded to very differently in different states. For example, the State of Pennsylvania already has closed down its state A-95 clearinghouse, and the Indiana legislature passed a bill invalidating regionalism of all types within its bounds. Fortunately, the Governor vetoed this bill, but its favorable reception in the legislature shows how unlikely it is that substate regions in Indiana will receive a boost from that source.

On the other hand, the Florida legislature passed a brand new substate districting act in 1980 setting forth a number of specific state goals and objectives to be met with the explicit help of the state's regional planning bodies. At the same time, Minnesota was surveying its regions and its departments of state government to inventory all of the instances of joint activities existing between these two levels of government as well as those having potential for development in the future.

As federal aid increasingly comes in the form of block grants, the states will gain new powers for the distribution of federal funds within their boundaries. In some of the pre-existing federal aid programs, regional planning played a large role in allocating funds among local governments. It remains to be seen whether the states will elect to use regional organizations in this manner under the new block grants. Some such programs are mental health, alcohol and drug abuse, nutrition, child development and day care, social services, and community action. It is likely that some states will continue to use the regional approach in these programs, while others will not.

The message is clear. Regionalism still has a good chance to thrive in those states where the state government desires to make use of it. In other states, the regional organizations may do well simply to survive. Interstate metropolitan areas, in particular, may have very little external support.

The Advisory Commission on Intergovernmental Relations (ACIR) has provided model legislation to underpin a strong substate districting system within any state desiring to enact it. This bill mandates regional planning, helps to pay for it, establishes a project notification and review process similar to the federal government's A-95 requirement, urges interstate cooperation, and provides other means by which regional councils can be effective.

In those states without such legislation, substate regional councils may have little choice but to take on a survival mode of operation. They may seek to charge fees for their publications and data, to cut their staff size very substantially, to set strict priorities for pursuing only those activities most essential to their survival, and to seek out all means of squeezing higher productivity from every expenditure they make. In short, they will have to practice cut-back management very seriously.

In many of these cut-back situations, the organization may become little more than the secretariat to a group of policy, technical, and citizen advisory committees. This is the stage at which many regional planning organizations were 15 or 20 years ago. Even at this level, however, the organization can perform its most essential function; namely, keeping areawide communications alive. Maintaining a project review function, regardless of the fate of OMB Circular A-95, plus continuing to provide data services and technical assistance, even if fees must be charged, appear to be the most likely and essential roles. In contrast, the preparation of ambitious plans probably will not continue in many regions during the next few years.

Regional councils may huddle closer together in their state associations, 37 of which now have been formed (ACIR, forthcoming). They certainly would be well advised to do so, as the states increasingly come to hold the keys to their success. At the very least, the councils need positive state recognition and shared purposes. On a national average, the states have increased their funding of regional budgets by about 10 percent; with effective lobbying this may be increased.

The bottom line, most probably, is that regional planning organizations will survive in most metropolitan areas and in a large number of nonmetropolitan ones as well, but they no longer will be supported in the style to which they have grown accustomed. Most will have to scratch out their existence in much less fertile fields than before.

PART THREE

Functional Issues

4. Regional Solid Waste Management Planning

Patrick J. Holland

INTRODUCTION

During the last ten years, the problem of managing the solid wastes generated by human activity has caused mounting concern and action in the United States. Management of solid wastes is increasingly a regional activity, requiring planning and implementation strategies which realistically address the opportunities and constraints inherent in a diverse institutional environment.

The purpose of this paper is to examine solid waste management planning in Cuyahoga County, Ohio since 1976. These solid waste management activities were a direct result of Public Law 94-580, the Resource and Conservation Recovery Act of 1976 (RCRA). What began as a substate planning activity, pursuant to the mandate of RCRA, turned into project development for a solid waste disposal facility. Although a needed resource recovery facility is to be constructed, regional planning failed to provide comprehensive measures to solve the problem of solid waste management in the region. This paper will also review some of the major plan implementation problems experienced by the Cuyahoga County project which are not unique to solid waste management as a regional activity.

41

REGIONAL SOLID WASTE MANAGEMENT

Solid waste management is the systematic control of the collection, storage, transportation, separation, processing, recovery, and disposal of solid waste. Although the collection and transportation of this waste is an integral part of solid waste management, this paper will address only the disposal aspect.

Traditionally, solid waste management has been undertaken by local governments in response to the need to protect the public health and the environment. Disposal of solid waste becomes a regional issue when a community or its agent is unable to utilize a suitable disposal option within its own boundary. The resulting imposition of one community's waste upon another necessitates a regional approach to the management of solid waste disposal.

The solid waste management problem has been most acute in the urbanized regions of the United States, where the combination of large solid waste volumes, few environmentally acceptable disposal sites, and increasing transportation and disposal costs has produced a crisis condition for local governments. These urban areas are generally characterized by significant institutional and political fragmentation, which impedes effective regional planning and plan implementation. The examination of opportunities and constraints relating to regional solid waste management planning must begin with a review of federal involvement since 1976.

THE FEDERAL PERSPECTIVE—THE RCRA

The Resource Conservation and Recovery Act (RCRA) of 1976 prompted the development of regional institutional structures to deal with the disposal issue. Subtitle D of RCRA provided for the identification of areas which have common solid waste management problems and are appropriate units for planning regional solid waste management services. Subtitle D also provides for the preparation of state solid waste management plans. A minimum requirement for state plans is the identification of the responsibilities of state, local, and regional entities in implementing the state plan, and the means for coordinating regional planning and implementation.

Section 4006 of Subtitle D specifies the procedure to be used for the development and implementation of a state plan. Paragraph B of this section calls for the identification of solid waste functions to be conducted by regional or local authorities. Whenever feasible, planning agencies designated pursuant to Section 208 of the Federal Water Pollution Control Act Amendments of 1972 (P.L. 92-500) are to be considered desirable solid waste planning agencies. This reference to Section 208 Water Quality Agencies suggests that solid waste management is to be conducted on a comprehensive regional planning and implementation basis.

Nevertheless, there are problems inherent in any attempt at planning and implementation at the regional level. In politically and institutionally fragmented urban areas, the actual planning and implementation which results from federal and state mandates often bears only a slight resemblance to the process originally envisioned. The tension between the federal bias toward generalized areawide planning and the local bias toward planning as a focused contributor to management at the operational level has created confusion, not effective and comprehensive planning. The experience of Cuyahoga County is an illustration.

REGIONAL PERSPECTIVE—PLANNING VS. IMPLEMENTATION

In Cuyahoga County, the distinction between planning and implementation became confused from the very outset. Cuyahoga County is a part of the Cleveland Standard Metropolitan Statistical Area and encompasses the City of Cleveland, 55 other municipal corporations, and four townships within about 453 square miles along 30 miles of the south shore of Lake Erie.

In Ohio, county government is an entity created by the state constitution; its powers are limited to those expressly granted by the state constitution and Ohio statutes. County government consists of a three-member board of commissioners, elected at-large, and the various departments and agencies created to administer county responsibilities. In contrast, the 56 municipalities within the county are vested with broad home-rule powers and responsibility for the protection of the public health and welfare, including solid waste management.

In 1980, the census reported one and one-half million persons living within Cuyahoga County. Recent studies indicate a per capita solid waste generation of approximately 2.8 pounds per day; at this rate, 763,000 tons per year of municipal solid waste is produced and must be collected, transported, and disposed of in an environmentally acceptable and cost-effective manner. In addition, an equal amount of commercial and industrial solid waste is generated in the area.

The need to develop a solid waste management plan for Cuyahoga County and to find alternatives to landfill disposal was demonstrated by an Ohio Environmental Protection Agency (Ohio EPA) survey of solid waste practices in 1976. One of the survey determinations was that the 56 municipalities and four townships in Cuyahoga County faced an impending municipal solid waste disposal crisis due to the limitations of existing landfills within the urban area. Both disposal costs at existing landfills and the costs of transporting waste increasing distances were rising rapidly.

Six months before the enactment of the RCRA in September 1976, the Ohio EPA contracted with a private consulting firm to review solid waste management practices in Ohio. Its report, issued in November 1976, was to be the basis for Ohio EPA's assistance to local officials in evaluating solid waste management options and for subsequent planning (Stanley Consultants, 1976).

In July 1977, the Ohio EPA again employed the consulting firm to develop an implementation plan to recover energy and resources from municipal solid waste generated in an urban county. Cuyahoga County was chosen as the study area for this implementation plan, or Phase II, of the the RCRA state plan. The implementation plan was completed in August 1978. It consisted of a detailed solid waste inventory, evaluation of energy and material markets, site and transportation analyses, environmental impact evaluation, and a project management plan (Stanley Consultants, 1978). Therefore, because of its concern about the disposal practices in areas that had limited landfill availability, the Ohio EPA had completed major elements of the state plan before RCRA became law or the RCRA regulations were fully developed.

In May 1978, when the Cuyahoga County implementation plan was three-quarters completed, the governor of Ohio designated the Cuyahoga County Regional Planning Commission as the planning agency pursuant to Section 4006 of the RCRA. Concurrently, the governor designated the Cuyahoga County Board of Commissioners as the implementation agency.

Before the governor's designation, however, a brief but intense struggle for the RCRA planning and implementation agency designations occurred between popularly elected county officials and the Northeast Ohio Areawide Coordinating Agency (NOACA). The NOACA is the Cleveland area A-95 metropolitan clearinghouse and 208 Water Quality Planning Agency for a five county area consisting of one urban county and four surrounding rural or suburban counties. The Cuyahoga County commissioners contended that the urban-rural dichotomy created real obstacles to fashioning integrated solutions which were cost-effective for both areas. Additionally, a combination of factors such as a large and relatively concentrated supply of solid waste, an extensive energy market, and a disposal problem approaching crisis proportions, suggested that Cuyahoga County had a singular opportunity to develop a resource recovery facility. There was also a strong belief among Cuyahoga County officials that the NOACA tended to regard federal programs and regulations, rather than the population and popularly elected governmental entities in the area, as its sole constituency. The NOACA contended that the RCRA called for the designation of the area's 208 Water Quality Agency. The conflict was settled upon the governor's designation of the Cuyahoga County Regional Planning Commission and the Cuyahoga County commissioners. The governor designated the NOACA as the planning agency for the balance of the water quality planning area. The split-planning designation was the first instance of a shift from substate regional planning to project implementation.

The Regional Planning Commission negotiated a three-phase, three-year contract with the Ohio EPA and began plan development in September 1978. In May 1979, the United States Environmental Protection Agency (USEPA) notified the Ohio EPA that federal pass-through funding was not to be used for substate planning activities. The Ohio EPA instructed the Regional Planning Commission to compress the imcomplete planning activities into a time space that would meet the funding level that had been committed by the State for the balance of the year. Thus, because of severe Ohio EPA budget limitations and the inability to use federal pass-through funds, the substate regional planning approach in Cuyahoga County area ended soon after it began, and total emphasis was shifted from solid waste management planning to implementation activities. From the federal viewpoint, solid waste management planning was out, and facility implementation and construction was in.

In October 1978, the USEPA announced a financial assistance program for resource recovery project development as part of the President's Urban Policy. The financial assistance program was designed to help cities move effectively through a project planning and development process which would result in timely and successful construction of facilities. Ironically, the program announcement noted that many states had not completed the planning process mandated by Section 4006 of the RCRA.

The Cuyahoga County Board of Commissioners, the designated implementation agency, applied for and was awarded planning funds for the implementation of a resource recovery facility to serve the muncipalities within the county. The Regional Planning Commission became a subcontractor to the implementation agency and subsequently performed some of the planning tasks identified in the original substate plan scope of work.

Although the Ohio EPA had begun its solid waste management activities before the advent of the RCRA and was committed to rapid progress from planning through project implementation, the U.S. Congress stressed substate regional planning patterned after the Section 208 Water Quality Planning model. Although it was not widely articulated at the time, weaknesses in the federally inspired regional planning process caused a shift in federal policy. The problems the USEPA was experiencing with the 208 planning model subsequently became the subject of examination and resulted in a reduction of federal funding (Edgmon, 1979). The change in policy was accomplished by the realignment of USEPA funding priorities. Funding was withdrawn from substate planning and funneled to project implementation, primarily in urban areas. It can be surmised that urban projects met the political priorities of the time. The impact of this policy shift has yet to be felt in Cuyahoga County.

The county's resource recovery facility, currently in the full service contractor procurement phase, is scheduled to be operational in 1987. It is being sized to dispose of 80 percent of the municipal waste generated in Cuyahoga County. Projections indicate little or no landfill capacity will exist within the county in 1987. How the commercial and industrial waste generated within the county in 1987 will be disposed of is a problem that is yet to be considered. It is reasonable to assume that if the regional planning process had been allowed to be completed, the problem of managing these wastes would have been addressed.

Whether a comprehensive regional solid waste management plan could have been implemented in Cuyahoga County, given the existing institutional and political barriers, is indeterminate. What is known, however, is that in the case of solid waste management involving the federal, state, and local governments, project implementation was the winner over regional planning.

THE POLITICS OF SOLID WASTE MANAGEMENT

Despite the involvement of the USEPA and the State of Ohio, solid waste management planning and implementation remain local responsibilities, and politics remains a basic ingredient in local decision making. A discussion of the political element is essential to surveying the opportunities and constraints inherent in solid waste management.

As previously indicated, Cuyahoga County is made up of 56 incorporated municipalities and four unincorporated townships. Because of the strong home rule charters in incorporated municipalities in Ohio, the Board of County Commissioners has direct powers in the four small townships only. As a result, 56 mayors, 413 city council members, 12 township trustees, 60 law directors, 60 service directors, three city managers, and three county commissioners are potentially involved in the solid waste planning and decision-making processes. Excluding appointed officials, this decision-making group totals 484 people.

Historically, there has been little joint planning or implementation among the 60 communities, especially among the central city, Cleveland, and the surrounding suburbs. In many instances, there has been overt hostility regarding regional infrastructure management, particularly the wastewater and water systems. Extensive litigation occurred in 1972 regarding the rate structure and operation of Cleveland's wastewater treatment system, resulting in the creation of a Regional Sewer Authority by the Common Pleas Court. As a result of litigation initiated in 1976 by the suburban communities concerning the city's operation of the water systems, the same court mandated a massive capital improvement program to be undertaken by Cleveland.

Political jealousies run deep. Suburban officials are resentful of the amount of funding the central city receives from federal and state agencies, as well as the attention of the media. Cleveland politicians resent suburban criticism and interference in Cleveland municipal operations, although many of these operations directly affect suburban constituencies. Although the conviction is not well articulated, Cleveland politicians believe that suburban communities foster the flight of population and employment from the central city, thereby reducing the tax base needed to support governmental services.

Despite these parochial attitudes and relationships, the development of a disposal facility serving the needs of Cleveland and the suburbs is inching forward. The major project milestones which must be accomplished during the implementation stage of a resource recovery facility project, such as obtaining long-term waste stream commitments, selecting the energy market and site, defining the financing options, and choosing procurement methods and mode of operations management, are difficult to complete.

The siting of the resource recovery facility provides a good example of how the planning process interacts with the decision-making process in the existing political environment. Much of the site selection planning was performed by the Regional Planning Commission as subcontractor to the Board of County Commissioners. The planning criteria for site selection included factors such as proximity of the site to the energy markets, logistics of transporting waste to the site, surrounding land uses, zoning, and environmental impacts. A site which meets all the technical criteria was recommended and was selected by both the planning and implementation agencies.

Nevertheless, opposition from some suburban and several Cleveland City Council officials surfaced. Suburban officials objected that the site was too distant and because of increased hauling costs, created an economic hardship on their communities. Some Cleveland City Councilmen protested that the Cleveland site would be a garbage dump for wealthy suburbs. The real basis for suburban concern has been the fear that, because the city would be purchasing the electricity generated, Cleveland would in some manner gain a disproportionate benefit from the facility. Suburban officials also fear that Cleveland will gain operating control of the facility, even though the facility is being procured on a full service basis; that is, one firm will be selected to design, construct, and operate the facility during a 20-year period.

The Cleveland City Council's opposition is based upon two unspoken factors. A recently adopted charter revision requires that the council be immediately reduced from 33 to 21 members, forcing several incumbents to campaign against one another. Campaign issues were scarce, and the proposed siting of a garbage burner was the answer to a politician's prayer. Moreover, several council members are concerned about the resource recovery facility's impact upon local waste haulers, a group with a traditionally effective lobby.

The political impediments to project implementation are being overcome because of the leadership of one individual with exceptional popularity and credibility among both Cleveland and suburban voters, the Mayor of the City of Cleveland.[1] The Mayor's involvement is not lip service, but aggressive action *vis-à-vis* the City Council, suburban officials, and the media.

As a result of the political fragmentation that commonly exists on a substate regional level or on a metropolitan level, plan implementation is extremely difficult to achieve. Planning can inspire and contribute to the solution of difficult problems. However, this will only come about if effective political leadership exists and is able to adopt plans and force their implementation.

In a politically fragmented area, the alternative to plan implementation by means of local political leadership is the intervention by a state authority which has the power to mandate siting, control the flow of municipal waste to a facility, and has the ability to provide financing. The creation of such state authorities marks a trend, examples of which include the Delaware Solid Waste Authority, the Louisiana Resource Recovery and Development Authority, and the Wisonsin Solid Waste Recycling Authority. Other states have created agencies with somewhat more limited but still substantial powers, for example the California Solid Waste Management Board, the Connecticut Resources Recovery Authority, and the Rhode Island Solid Waste Management Corporation.

The elimination of local responsibility for solid waste management, while a valid alternative, raises serious questions of governance which merit full examination. Given the instability of local political leadership, such an examination may conclude that intervention by a state authority may be the only viable means to bring about cost-effective and environmentally acceptable solid waste management.

5. Coastal Zone Management: Planning for an Environmental Region

Alden McLellan, IV and Brian D. Boxer

INTRODUCTION

The year 1980, designated by the President of the United States as The Year of the Coast, ended with the election of an administration that may terminate federal involvement in management of the nation's coastal zone. Coastal zone management, like many types of regional planning programs across the nation, is facing a threatening situation in which both federal regulation and financial supports are being withdrawn. It has long been suggested that the private sector can provide for the use of scarce resources in a manner which is both more socially efficient and less costly than governmental regulation. Federal policy in the years to come will attempt to apply this philosophy to management of our national coastal zone.

The purpose of this paper is to provide an understanding of the development and past contributions of coastal zone management and to develop a framework for viewing the future management of the coastal zone region. The nature of the coastal zone as a distinct region in need of a unique type of planning process is examined first. The history and institutional development of coastal zone management in the United States is presented next and is followed by a case study of the development of the coastal management program in the State of New Jersey. The New Jersey program, while far from perfect, is one of the most comprehensive programs of its type in the nation. Finally, the chapter will discuss the impact of current federal policy and budgetary restrictions on coastal zone management nationwide.

THE COASTAL ZONE

The coastal zone, the interface between the land, the sea, and the atmosphere, is a region that is biologically, geographically, economically, and demographically unique. The *Federal Coastal Zone Management Act of 1972* (P.L. 92-583) defined the coastal zone as "the coastal waters and the adjacent shorelands strongly influenced by each other and in proximity to the shorelines of the several coastal states, and includ(ing) transitional and intertidal areas, salt marshes, wetlands, and beaches." The coastal zone consists of the entire Great Lakes and ocean shoreline of the United States. It reaches inland only as far as is needed to manage coastal shorelands whose use impacts coastal waters. Some scholars have attempted to emphasize the ecological nature of the coastal zone. For example, Ditton, Seymour, and Swanson (1977) state that the coastal zone is the region where, for both human activities and natural ecosystems, "production, consumption, and energy exchange processes are most intense".

Pressures for development in the coastal zone have, in many areas, put the future of this important region in question. It has always been a characteristic of American cities, and human settlements in general, to be located on bodies of water in order to facilitate trade. Thus, development in the American coastal zone intensified rapidly as urbanization became a dominant social phenomenon in the Twentieth Century. By 1970 nearly 70 percent of the U.S. population resided within 50 miles of the ocean and Great Lakes shoreline (Ditton, Seymour, and Swanson, 1977, p. 4). It is projected that by 1990 as much as 75 percent of the American population will live within the coastal zone itself (Chasis, 1979, p. 274). A tremendous amount of pressure is thereby being placed on this very delicate coastal environment.

In addition to the ecological problems that the coastal zone faces due to intense population pressure, there are also efficiency and equity questions specific to the coast. Will planning intervention into the coastal zone result in a more or less efficient use of the resources that are available? What is the role of equity in planning for the use of coastal resources? If one accepts the premise that any intervention is biased toward some segment of the population, decisions must be made as to who will benefit disproportionately from coastal zone management. For example, there is a carrying capacity for any land system, and therefore the coastal zone has a limit to the number of people that can use it without causing serious damage. Unregulated, coastal property would be acquired by the highest bidder, thus excluding a majority of the population from use of this resource. Coastal zone management intervenes in this market-like system. Development permits and public access requirements allow a more diverse group to use the coastal zone, altering the distribution that the market might provide.

Finally, the question of how to use the coastal zone must be faced. Many uses may be more efficient today but could cause ecological disaster tomorrow. Given the value of coastal areas to the populous, some sort of regulation is called for to determine valid uses of the region.

The coastal zone is, indeed, a distinct region, important to the ecological health and economic vitality of our nation. The coastal zone is a region which stretches for thousands of miles along a very thin strip at the nation's edge. In this sense, national direction and coordination of coastal zone management may be most appropriate. However, the coastal zone is so diverse that one could envision hundreds of small regional planning agencies. The latter situation, one of extreme political decentralization and fragmentation, is precisely the problem that regional planning is trying to solve. The compromise has been a type of environmental federalism. Each state has been allowed to develop a regional planning body and program for its individual section of the coastal region. While this situation is probably not the best possible situation, use of the existing institutional framework at the state level has facilitated more rapid program development than could be anticipated otherwise. Not to ignore the true regional nature of the coastal zone, provisions in the federal process encourage and provide funds for interstate cooperation and coordination. This approach to regulation of the coastal region appears to have been successful.

DEVELOPING A CONSENSUS FOR COASTAL MANAGEMENT

Active federal involvement in the coastal zone management process began in 1966 with the authorization of a commission to study coastal zone problems. However, the problems that the coastal shoreline was facing, including possibly irreversible damage by irresponsible and uninformed users, had been a concern of the legislatures of coastal states and municipalities for many years. In the 1920s and 1930s, the legislative bodies of many coastal states began to provide financial and technical assistance to shorefront municipalities. This aid, which came at the request and urging of municipalities, was primarily intended to help deal with the problem of shoreline erosion. The 1940s saw some states formally authorize a state agency to establish a program to provide physical protection of the shoreline. Agencies of this type concentrated mainly on operations such as constructing and repairing seawalls, bulkheads, breakwaters, and jetties, providing beachfill, protecting sand dunes, and other related projects.

The 1950s and 1960s were decades which saw a growing conflict in concepts of appropriate uses of, and thus planning for, our nation's coastal zone. There had long been a great deal of emphasis on the theory that the resources of our nation were to be used in order to further economic development. The supremacy of this tenet during the post-World War II decades can be seem in many coastal communities across the nation; a prime example can be found in New Jersey where on the northern coastline, known as "the shore," many miles of sand dunes and precious barrier island environment were destroyed in order to build summer cottages and amusement piers. During this period coastal wetlands were converted to productive agricultural land at an alarming rate.

However, these same years also witnessed growing public awareness that unimpeded ecological destruction of the nation's coastline was to be questioned. The work of authors such as Rachel Carson helped increase public awareness of the value and the tenuous nature of a healthy environment. Carson, in *Silent Spring* (1962) and other works, showed a special interest in the coast and helped bring to the public's attention the dangers of the type of environmental damage brought on by overdevelopment.

The year 1969 was a pivotal year in the development of a concensus regarding the necessity of coastal zone management. The United States Commission on Marine Science, Engineering, and Resources, the Stratton Commission, which had been authorized in

1966 to explore the specific problems of the coastal zone and to propose possible solutions, issued its report, *Our Nation and The Sea* (U.S. Commission on Marine Science, Engineering and Resources, 1969). The report emphasized the importance of the coastal zone as a national resource. It went so far as to state that "the coast of the United States is, in many respects, the Nation's most valuable geographic feature" (Leg. Hist. CZMA, 1976, p. 4). The report emphasized that the needs of the coastal zone had far outrun the capacities for development and planning for those local governments responsible for these tasks. The Stratton Commission suggested that "coastal zone management" was best performed at the state level under supervision of the National Oceanic and Atmospheric Administration (NOAA) (Leg. Hist. CZMA, 1976, p. 7).

Also in 1969, pursuant to an order in the Estuary Protection Act, the U.S. Department of the Interior issued the National Estuary Study. This study detailed the condition and different uses of American estuarine areas. It found that estuaries in the United States were being jeopardized by the pollution and physical damage produced by both individual and residential overdevelopment (Leg. Hist. CZMA, 1976, p. 7).

Perhaps no other single event helped coalesce sentiment in favor of coastal zone management so much as the 1969 oil spill off the coast of Santa Barbara, California. Television coverage of this disaster brought the realities of environmental abuse into each and everyone's living rooms. Protest was widespread. The following years saw the enactment of environmental protection laws at all levels of government, much of which emphasized protection of the nation's coastal zone.

THE COASTAL ZONE MANAGEMENT ACT

The Coastal Zone Management Act of 1972 (CZMA) was to become the basis for the federal coastal management effort. It was the culmination of many years of work by many people; yet it was just a beginning. The act established a national policy "to preserve, protect, develop, and where possible, to restore or enhance, the resources of the Nation's coastal zone for this and succeeding generations." The act did not, nor did it attempt to, establish a single national coastal zone management program. Rather, it sought to foster the development of regional programs administered by appropriate state agencies. The act stated that it is national policy to encourage and assist the states to exercise effectively their responsibilities in the coastal zone through the development and implementation of management programs to achieve the use of the land and water resources of the coastal zone giving full consideration to ecological, cultural, historic, and esthetic values as well as needs for economic development. (Leg. Hist. CZMA, 1976, p. 5).

In response to the growing concern over the future of the coastal zone, the act emphasized the importance of the coastal region. "The coastal zone is rich in a variety of natural, commercial, recreational, industrial, and aesthetic resources of immediate and potential value to the present and future well-being of the Nation" (Leg. Hist. CZMA, 1976, p. 5). It went on to focus the blame on overdevelopment and unplanned growth by all types of users. The act concluded by emphasizing that

the key to more effective protection and use of the land and water resources of the coastal zone is to encourage the states to exercise their full authority over the lands and waters in the coastal zone, assisting the states, in cooperation with Federal and local governments and other vitally affected interests, in developing land and water programs for the coastal zone, including unified policies, criteria, standards, methods, and processes for dealing with land and water use decisions of more than local significance.

The act mandated that each state develop a coastal management program which includes:

1. Clearly defined coastal zone boundaries;
2. A definition of coastal land and water uses which impact coastal waters;
3. An inventory of areas of special concern;
4. Identification of the legal and regulatory basis for enforcement of restrictions on uses listed in subsection 2 (above);
5. Clarification of the priority of potential uses for specific areas; and
6. A clearly defined organizational structure aimed at implementation of the management program. (Baram, 1976. p. 163).

Under Section 306 of the act, the federal government has been able to provide up to 80 percent of the funds needed for plan development. Other sections of the act also authorize federal financial support for coastal management-related interstate planning and research and technical aid for individual programs. Encouragement of interstate planning for coastal management purposes recognizes the regional nature of the problem. The act also makes federal money available for land acquisition in order to increase public access to the shoreline, to develop environmental sanctuaries, and to help preserve important coastal resources (Heikoff, 1980, p. 7).

The Coastal Zone Management Act was passed by Congress in 1972 and amended in 1974, 1976, and 1980. In those years we have moved closer to the time when the entire coastline of the U.S. will be under the jurisdiction of a federally approved coastal management program. It is important to step back and examine what institutional developments have been accomplished under the act.[1]

There are 35 coastal states and territories, and by 1980 each had been involved in the federal coastal zone management effort to some extent. At that time, 21 states had developed federally approved management programs with jurisdiction over at least 75 percent of the nation's coastline. Protection of the natural coastal environment is one of the main principles of coastal zone management. Eight of the 31 wetlands protection laws in existence in 1980 were enacted as a direct response to the federal mandate. In six coastal states, measures protecting endangered species have been included in coastal management programs, and of the 20 states with provisions for protection of "important, unique, or endangered flora and fauna," six have come as a result of the federal coastal zone management effort. According to Knecht (1979), 23 of the 35 coastal states have become involved in the protection of beaches, sand dunes, and barrier islands.

Coastal states are also taking steps to come to terms with the problems associated with coastal development. The major problems to be dealt with are erosion and sand dune destruction, energy facility siting, and use priorities for development. As of 1980, fourteen states had established setback requirements or preservation laws intended to prevent further geological damage to the coastal zone. Energy facility siting has been a volatile issue in many states, and by 1980 systems for dealing with this had been developed in twelve states. Additionally, eight states have established water-dependency as the primary determinant for the granting of a development permit.

The movement to gain greater public access to the shoreline was a major impetus behind the coastal zone management movement. Knecht suggests that increased public access is the key to the development of a greater constituency for the coastal management process. A requirement that access be provided, prior to issuance of a permit, can be found in nine states. Many states have instituted programs to gain public access to the shoreline through historic preservation statutes or through the creation of waterfront parks.

THE NEW JERSEY COASTAL MANAGEMENT PROGRAM

Coastal zone management in New Jersey has a long history dating back to 1821 when the New Jersey Supreme Court ruled in the case of *Arnold* v. *Mundy* that the state had the right to promote the general welfare through regulation of the state tidelands. The Waterfront Development Law of 1914 required state approval for "all plans for the development of any waterfront upon navigable water or stream . . . " In 1969 the passge of the Hackensack Meadowlands Reclamation and Development Act created a commission and required it to create a masterplan and oversee all development in the area.

A stepping stone to statewide coastal zone management came about in 1970 with the enactment of the Wetlands Act. This bill gave the New Jersey Department of Environmental Protection (DEP) the power to regulate all development in the state wetlands south of the Raritan River Basin. Finally, in 1973, the Coastal Area Facility Review Act (CAFRA) gave "DEP authority to regulate major development in the Bay and Ocean Shore Segment of the coastal zone to preserve environmentally sensitive sites and ensure a rational pattern of development" (NJDEP, 1980, p. 4).

Six years of policy development, from 1974 through 1980, culminated in federal approval of the *New Jersey Coastal Management Program and Final Environmental Impact Statement.* The New Jersey Coastal Management Program as it exists today is operated through the Division of Coastal Resources of the Department of Environmental Protection. Within the division there are five distinct bureaus. Prior to federal approval, the Bureau of Coastal Planning and Development had the task of developing the comprehensive program itself. Once federal approval was granted, the bureau took on the long term job of refining the projects and policies of the Coastal Management Program. The Bureau of Coastal Project Review administers the CAFRA, Wetlands, and Waterfront Development permit programs. It is this bureau which investigates and passes judgment on each of the applications. The Bureau of Tidelands aids in protection of the state-owned tidelands. The Bureau of Coastal Enforcement and Field Services is an inspection team that assists the Bureau of Tidelands and the Bureau of Coastal Project Review. Overseeing New Jersey's shore protection and waterway maintenance programs is the job of the Bureau of Coastal Engineering.

The program is regulatory in nature and is administered by the N.J. Departments of Environmental Protection and Energy, and by the Hackensack Meadowlands Development Commission. It receives its authority to regulate land and water uses through these state laws: the Waterfront Development Law, the Wetlands Act, and the CAFRA.

The Waterfront Development Law requires the DEP to regulate the development of docks, wharves, piers, bulkheads, bridges, pipelines, cables, and moorings as well as other underwater structures along the waterfront. Additionally, state approval is required prior to "construction, reconstruction, structural alteration, relocation or enlargement of any building or other structure, of any excavation or landfill, and any change in the use of any building or other structure, or land or extension of use of land" in the waterfront area.

The Waterfront Development Law has jurisdiction outside of the CAFRA area and the Hackensack Meadowlands District, over "all tidal waterways and lands adjacent thereto up to the first property line, public road or railroad right-of-way generally parallel to the waterway, provided that the boundary is between 100 and 500 feet from the waterway." (NJDEP, 1980, p. 32).

The Wetlands Act of 1970 gives the DEP jurisdiction over use of the state's coastal wetlands. The act gives the Division of Coastal Resources authority over nearly every type of use of the state's coastal wetlands, which are defined as "those wetlands subject to tidal action along specified water bodies." According to the Division of Coastal Resources, enactment of this portion of the coastal management program has reduced the number of acres of wetlands filled annually from 1900 to 55. In 1979 less than one acre of regulated wetland was filled (NJDEP, 1980, p. 37).

The cornerstone of coastal zone management in New Jersey is the 1973 CAFRA which "authorizes DEP to regulate and approve the location, design and construction of major facilities in a 1,376 square mile coastal region . . . ." The types of facilities under CAFRA jurisdiction are electrical power plants including nuclear facilities, public developments including housing developments over 25 units, agricultural processing, mineral and chemical production, and marine terminals and storage facilities (NJDEP, 1980, p. 37).

Under Section 305 of the federal Coastal Zone Management Act, New Jersey has received funding for program development. Since approval of the portion of the New Jersey Coastal Zone under the CAFRA, the DEP has been eligible for Section 306 implementation funds. In 1979 this amounted to $800,000 and increased to $840,000 in 1980. Federal approval of the complete coastal management program in September 1980 resulted in the allocation of $2,000,000 of Section 306 funds to New Jersey.

New Jersey also receives federal funds through Section 308 of the CZMA, the Coastal Energy Impact Program. Since 1977, the first year of the program, New Jersey has been granted almost $2 million and loaned nearly $3 million to help deal with problems associated with coastal energy facilities.

Coastal zone management in New Jersey is not entirely funded by the federal government. The Beaches and Harbors Bond Act of 1977 approved $20 million to be invested in beach restoration, maintenance, and protection project.

EVALUATION

The national coastal management process has facilitated the development of coastal planning in each American state and territory. While some states continue to work on plan development, other states have fully operational coastal management programs. As of early 1981 twenty-five states and territories, controlling over 75 percent of the nation's shoreline, have developed federally approved coastal management plans. This is a substantial payoff from the federal investment made over the last eight years. Yet the success of the coastal management program is dependent not only on plan development but also on implementation. Since plans for 59 percent of the coastal zone have been approved during the last year or so, drastic federal cutbacks are sure to severely restrict the ability of states such as Louisiana, Florida, and New Jersey to attain full implementation of their programs. According to Michael Glazer who headed the Coastal Zone Management Program under the Carter Administration, "some states such as California and Washington have already had five years of federal support and can reasonably be expected to fund their own program even now" (Glazer, 1981).

There have been substantial obstacles that states have encountered in program development and implementation. Coastal zone management becomes, as does any planning effort, particularly complicated when the program has conflicting objectives. The federal CZMA establishes a national policy which, among other things, sets out to protect and to develop the nation's coastal zone. Many believe that there is an inherent conflict between these objectives. These same people argue that multiple-use management is not possible because there is a perception of a zero-sum game with each decision. However, there are areas where multiple-use management of common property resources has been established for decades. For example, the management philosophy of the National Park Service has been quite flexible and has gone through narrow stages in accentuation of the objectives of diverse constituencies. This type of evolutionary process has and will continue to occur for coastal zone management also.

Coastal management presents immediate problems because of the inherent difficulties in the integration of scientific analysis and collective decision making. Collective decisions about how to use coastal lands have been made for the past two centuries in one way or another, with or without scientific data and analysis. The collective decision-making process has gone on at all levels of government and has persisted throughout many changes in the broader issues facing society, yet the conflict has not changed.

One of the problems that one faces in integrating science and collective decision making has to do with the interdisciplinary nature of coastal resources management. In order to adequately deal with an issue such as beach erosion near high-rise oceanfront buildings, advice must be sought not only from fluid dynamicists, meteorologists, and ecologists, but a multitude of additional issues must be addressed such as construction safety, aesthetics, transportation and adjacent service. The amount of funding necessary for the project-by-project evaluations is not available at local levels. For extremely large undertakings, funds are often made available directly from federal sources. In most cases, though, the state carries the financial burden of the scientific investigation.

THE FUTURE OF COASTAL ZONE MANAGEMENT

The present federal adminstration is not nearly as sympathetic to coastal conservation issues as those of previous administrations. The next few years will see an entirely new look from the federal involvement in the coastal zone management process; in fact, the process itself will, most probably, be phased out. Not only is there not a legislative constituency strong enough to withstand the pressure from the Administration to cut back the coastal management process, but the legislature has suggested cutbacks in excess of those slated. The House Appropriations Committee provided only $5.21 million for the program, an amount $3.2 million less than the initial executive budget request and a stunning $46.37 million less than that provided in the 1981 budget. Since it can be safely said that appropriations for coastal zone management will not increase significantly in the coming years, it appears that, financially, state coastal management programs are on their own.

However, the federal climate is not one which finds success in stopping programs in their tracks. Rather, the wheels have been set to decrease the effectiveness of existing state coastal programs. The Department of the Interior in particular has attempted to usurp the power of individual coastal management programs, specifically in terms of planning for leases for offshore oil and gas exploration. In July 1981 the Department of Commerce, under pressure from the Department of the Interior, exempted offshore lease sales from requirements of the act which requires that any federal action "directly affecting" coastal waters must be "consistent" with state environment standards. This change will effectively "take away much of the state's power to review offshore oil and gas leasing plans" *(Business Week,* 1980). The State of California successfully challenged a number of proposed lease sales off its coast, but this was accomplished prior to the change in regulation. It appears that a ruling now would not be as favorable.

This new direction in federal involvement in coastal activities is in direct conflict with the philosophical basis of the act which emphasized federal-state cooperation, and, in fact, against the Administration's own guidelines for regulatory reform. This new focus is contrary to the NOAA's past position, the intent of congressional action, and the direction of judicial opinion. If coastal states are excluded from discussions concerning their coastlines, as is directed in the NOAA's new policies, the federal government will contradict its own philosophy toward federal-state relationships (Lerner, 1981).

CONCLUSION

Coastal zone management will survive the present adversities. Some individual programs will be hurt far more than others; it appears that those which had developed considerable state constituencies will continue, though at a less active level, while those programs not so firmly entrenched may lose much more of their previous effectiveness. The program in New Jersey will go on, but the loss of federal funding will decrease the budget by roughly 20 percent. It is the change of the federal government's attitude that is most threatening to coastal management programs. If the federal government continues the movement away from viewing the coastal zone as an important and ecologically unique and fragile environment, individual state coastal planning will be severely hindered regardless of the level of state commitment. Government at all levels must be brought to see the coastal zone as a distinct and important region, and to provide a planning network capable of successfully resolving the issues particular to it.

6. Planning and Economic Development

Roger J. Vaughan

INTRODUCTION

It is a fortuitous time to debate the role of regional planning.[1] The new economics of Washington is redefining both the role and the funding of regional planning organizations. Traditional federal sources of funding for planning activities appear to be drying up.[2] At the same time, the New Federalism is delegating a much greater fiscal and administrative responsibility for economic development policy to state governments. It is no exaggeration to say that planning as we have traditionally known it is passing through a dramatic transformation and it would be a courageous pundit who would predict the role of planning agencies during the next decade.

I would like to define my terms and basic assumptions. My concern in this paper is with the role of planning in economic development policy. I fully acknowledge the critical role of planners in the design of a specific project, such as a highway spur, a shopping mall, a waste water treatment plant, or an industrial park. I am much less certain that planners have, or should play, a role in the design and development of economic policy. Indeed, most economists fall into the same traps that ensnare planners and are unable to perform timely, realistic, and relevant analyses for policy makers.

Let us begin with a brief and oversimplified history of planning. In the 1920s, planners were reformers. They opposed sprawling, unhealthy, and unaesthetic urban development that was often shaped more by the land ownership patterns of local politicians than more solid economic rationale. Planning offered an alternative, and the concerns of planners led to comprehensive zoning ordinances, fire and health codes, and the integration of land use and transportation patterns. With a few notable exceptions in the Southwest, those battles have largely been won.

Rapid suburbanization gave a new cause to planning. As the automobile replaced the streetcar, and as single-family homes boomed after World War II, municipal and state governments needed to anticipate how to locate public facilities, from parks and libraries to water systems and schools, and planners were willing to supply attractive maps to service as blueprints for these efforts.

The third wave of planning gathered momentum as the volume of federal grants-in-aid increased. Each grant required a detailed application. Urban renewal, highways, waste water treatment plants, and Urban Development Action Grant (UDAG) projects all served to employ planners. Federal agencies, anxious to prove that their grants were not simply supplanting state and local spending, required applicants to prepare long-run plans which would establish the absolute necessity of the project for the long-run economic viability of the applicant jurisdiction, and the fiscal need for the federal resources. Planning moved into a central role in economic development policy. Examples of this are Overall Economic Development Plans, Committee for Economic Development (CED) plans, and numerous other efforts. Local planning was supported by the lead economic development agencies at the federal level—the Department of Housing and Urban Development (HUD) and the Economic Development Administration (EDA). These agencies were, in effect, creating a local constituency to ensure full and popular utilization of their own programs.

This somewhat cynically depicted, thumbnail sketch can be used as a backdrop against which to illustrate the fundamental weaknesses of planning as a tool in the development of economic policy. My conclusion is that planning as it has traditionally been taught and practiced has very little to offer to either the economic policy maker or the progam administrator. Policy analysis, the diagnosis of economic problems, is critical to economic policy. Planning, even the increasingly fashionable "strategic planning," is not useful.

This conclusion may seem harsh, and I will admit that in this paper I have erected something of a straw-man planner to attack. It may well be that the role of policy analysis that I outline is close to the concept that many of you have of planning. My conclusions do not rest upon a systematic and academically respectable survey of planning activities by a statistically selected sample of planning activities and agencies. My views have evolved while working with, and sometimes against, planners on many public policy issues and projects. Although my own office, the New York Office of Development Planning, includes the word "planning," I would be reluctant to hire a graduate of a planning department.

Following are the reasons behind what many will feel is an unduly restrictive view of the role of planning in economic policy. First, the planning discipline does not provide rigorous criteria for determining when public intervention in the economy is appropriate. Identification of a regional economic problem, persistent pockets of poverty, an abandoned plant, or slow income growth, does not, in itself, justify creating a public program to address the problem. That can only be done when the causes of the problem are diagnosed and the effectiveness of alternative policies evaluated. These tasks are the work of economists, not planners. Economists have developed the concept of market failure to determine, on efficiency grounds, when public intervetion may be appropriate. They have also developed cost-benefit techniques as a basis for program evaluation.

Accurate diagnosis and evaluation require a model of the process of economic development. A second flaw with planning and with a great deal of economics is that the discipline largely ignores the dynamic process of economic development and, instead, focuses upon the comparison of two static equilibria states. There is little attention paid to how the regional economy might move from one state to the other, how much the adjustment might cost, nor whether the final state would be relevant if it were reached.

Third, planners are usually far removed from the operational side of policies and programs. This severly limits the usefulness of policy recommendations because such recommendations rarely include any analysis of either:

1. Inadvertent side effects of the policy on the development process, or
2. the institutional issues in the design and execution of the policy, or
3. the political environment in which decisions are made and which necessitate the identification of possible second-best trade-offs in advance.

Finally, because of the inflexibility of planning within the framework of policy analysis and development, planners are normally far removed from the decision-making process. This means that planners are rarely able to identify priorities, anticipate policy concerns, or to provide analysis that is useful for the policy process.

I would repeat that many of the failings of planning as an academic discipline are also failings of academic economists. But economists, because they have developed a more useful conceptual framework for understanding economic development, have been able to identify relationships between public policy and economic behavior that have, in some instances, helped shape policy debate.[3] Planning, lacking a conceptual framework, has proved less useful.

A clear illustration of the weakness of planning in developing economic policy can be seen in the desire a few years ago by local planning agencies to stimulate local economies by identifying "growth industries." A great deal of enthusiasm and computer time was expended examining growth performance, factor requirements, interindustry links, and any other arcane data, usually at the four digit Standard Industrial Classification (SIC) level, that might yield the secret of predicting local industry growth. Yet I question whether these exercises were of more than marginal policy relevance. Predicting the growth prospect of an industry, however accurately, yields no information on what policy levers might be pulled to influence it nor on how responsive the industry would be to those policies. The numerous, thick studies are now memorials to the futility of planning without regard to policy.

The following sections of the paper will first briefly outline the relationship between economic development and economic policy. Second, a dynamic approach to policy analysis and development will be described. And finally, some ways in which planning activities can be integrated more effectively into the policy process will be discussed.

ECONOMIC DEVELOPMENT AND ECONOMIC POLICY

Although economic issues have become top priorities at all levels of government, there is considerable confusion over exactly what economic development is and even more confusion over what the public sector can do about it.

One way to define a basic concept is to state what it is not. Economic development is not simply economic growth. Development is both a prerequisite to and result of growth. The two terms differ in that development is a qualitative change which entails changes in the structure of the economy including innovations in institutions, behavior, and technology. Growth, on the other hand, is a quantitative change in the scale of the economy in terms of investment, output, consumption, and income.

Growth cannot long continue without the sort of innovations and structural changes implicit in development. However, as with any other useful distinction, the differences which appear sharp in concept are less sharp in reality. There are circumstances under which growth might appear to cause development. In a dynamic economy, a host of minor developmental changes will accompany growth in output. Enterprises and households adapt incrementaly in response to changing incomes, demands, prices, and other decision-determining parameters. As these incremental changes accumulate, they find that the increasing scale and diversification of the economy cause problems that cannot be dealt with by minor adaptations. Major innovations or structural changes are called for. If they do not occur or they occur too slowly, the economy then enters a period of no-or-slow growth until those basic institutional adjustments are made.

Development can also arise independently of growth through exogenous forces or shocks such as the recent increase in energy prices, and through major scientific and technological changes. These shocks or changes induce development by creating disequilibrium conditions in the economy, conditions that necessitate major institutional and structural change.

The purpose of economic policy is not to return the economy to some defined equilibrium state, or even to steer the economy toward some hypothetical future equilibrium state, but to facilitate the process of adjustment. Unfortunately, the typical policy response to an economic problem is to try to wind back the economic clock. The urban crisis of the mid-1970s spawned many programs designed to bring manufacturing jobs back to the central city. The reindustrialization crisis today has led to proposals such as the Reconstruction Finance Corporation, the principal impact of which would be to shore up old, large and declining corporations at the expense of new firms embodying state-of-the-art production techniques. This is a typical public policy response, all too often the result of planning for economic development.

Schumpeter has pointed out that, in a market economy, this disequilibrium-dynamic process of development involves a process of "creative destruction." Old resources are devalued and new resources revalued. Some industries, institutions, and areas lead and some lag in the uneven process of economic development. Contrary to the economic textbooks, the disequilibrium nature of the process is not only endemic to a dynamic market economy, it is necessary for the continual regeneration of entrepreneurship. This description also differs from the traditional view of economic progress, in which the national and local economies march inexorably and in step along a growth path. Decline, devaluation, and disinvestment in some areas and industries is the necessary counterpart of growth in other areas. For areas whose products were in demand during the last stage of development, the adjustments can be painful.

If we accept this dynamic view of the economy, then designing economic policy must focus on the development process and not try to impose a development plan. Each element will only prove effective if it is based on a sound understanding of the dynamics of development and how we can best speed the adjustment process.

The overall goal of development strategy should be to facilitate dynamic adjustments. Within the context of this goal, the four specific objectives are:

1.　To increase the level or rate of growth of economic activity;
2.　To target economic activity toward economically distressed communities;
3.　To enhance opportunities for the economically disadvantaged; and
4.　To improve the quality of jobs by, for example, increasing wages, improving working conditions, or reducing cyclical instability.

Translated into employment terms, economic policy may be concerned with the level of employment, the location of employment, who gets the jobs, or the types of jobs created.

BARRIERS TO ECONOMIC DEVELOPMENT

The purpose of economic policy is to reduce or abolish the barriers that prevent successful adaptation to economic change. If there were no barriers, the communities would not suffer from structural unemployment. Local employees rendered jobless by the decline of an industry would have moved into other occupations which foresight had allowed them to prepare for in advance. But markets do not operate in this way. Uncertainty, imperfect information, and relocation costs are just some of the factors which impede adaptation.

This section reviews these barriers and the implications of this framework for policy development. The first part examines some of the basic operation of markets themselves, and those that have resulted from public intervention, such as regulations and taxation. Then the section reviews the implications for economic policy development.

Market Failure and Development Policy

Factors of production are mainly sold through markets. For some factors, the markets are clearly defined; for some they are not. The price of labor is determined by negotiation between employers and workers, sometimes on an individual basis, sometimes for entire work forces. Land is sold through the competitive bidding among purchasers. Other markets are less clearly defined. Amenities are rarely sold directly but are reflected in the price a purchaser is willing to offer for a location with attractive features such as clean air and ready access to recreational space. Publicly provided services are implicitly sold and the price is the local tax rate. Some markets are ill-defined because they are internal, that is, job channels within firms or business services are provided in-house.

The purpose of the market is to send signals to the participants to indicate when they need to change their behavior and to indicate the direction of the appropriate change. The employer who fails to fill vacant slots is receiving a signal to raise wages. A job seeker who fails to find employment is receiving a signal either to seek elsewhere, to reduce expectations, or to acquire more marketable skills.

When markets work well, the right signals are sent out and the economy responds rapidly to changes. That does not mean that no firms close down or that no one is out of work. Microinstability is necessary for adaptation. Innovative young firms introduce new products and new production techniques that replace older firms. Increasing energy costs lead to a decline in the output of energy-intensive products and shifts in transportation patterns. Increasing the rate of investment in new plants and equipment requires some disinvestment in old plants and equipment.

To the economist, the definition of the public sector role in economic development traditionally proceeds from a specification of private market failures. The following are the diagnoses for these failures:

1.   Imperfect Information—The unemployed worker does not know where there are job openings, or the investor does not have enough information to assess the viability of a project.

2.   Transactions Costs—The cost of relocation may prevent an unemployed worker from moving to a growing labor market, or the costs of a bond issue may make an investment nonviable.

3.   Increasing Returns to Scale—An economic activity, such as a job referral service, may be the cheapest if performed nationwide, yet no single private company can capture these economies. Similarly, a very large venture capital corporation would undertake risky projects because its overall portfolio is diversified. A small company will not undertake as much risk on any single project because it is not as diversified (Daniels and Kieschnick, 1978).

4.   Externalities—An activity that generates spillover benefits that do not accrue to those paying for the activity will not be undertaken at an optimal level. For example, basic research will not be adequately funded privately because the sponsor will be able to appropriate only a small part of the benefits. A firm will be reluctant to pay for non-job-specific training for an employee because that employee can leave for another company.

5.   Second-Best—An imperfection in one market will lead to imperfections in related markets. If capital is denied to high-risk enterprises, then the level of employment in the high-risk sector will be below the socially optimal.

6. Public Intervention—Collecting taxes or regulating eco-
    nomic activity will distort the operations of markets. For
    example, taxing income discourages labor force participa-
    tion. Regulating minimum wages reduces the number of
    low-wage jobs.
7. Market Power—If markets are insufficiently competitive,
    then a good service or factor will be priced inefficiently
    high and incentives for product or process innovation will
    be weak.

For many purposes, this classification is useful. Yet, several relevant failures or barriers to development are missing or incom-
pletely specified. The market failure concept is too static. Most failures are defined as deviations from the ideal and totally unrealistic
model of perfect competition, which is a model of static, not dynamic efficiency. In a dynamic market economy, there will be a
tendency for market imperfections to diminish since some entre-
preneurial types can profit from providing a good or service which
remedies the fault. If the failure persists, then it must have some
functional roles in maintaining the market system, in which case
the term "failure" is inappropriate. But this presumes a supply of
entrepreneurs to develop these new products and that these entrepreneurs do face incentives to bridge market gaps. The persistence
of failures signifies a lack of entrepreneurs or that public interven-
tions is acting as a barrier to development.

The second major failing of the simple market failure analysis is
its implicit suggestion that the best way to foster development is to
remove all impediments to the normal functioning of a market
economy. This assumes not only that all development resources are
bought, sold, and produced in private markets, but that the latter
are self-organizing and self-perfectible. Rather than reflect further
on the unreality of this viewpoint, let us specify some additional
barriers to the dynamically efficient creation and utilization of resources for development.

1. Lack of Entrepeneurship—Without individuals with access
    to capital and familiar with business management who are
    willing to take risks and identify market gaps, new enter-
    prises will not be set up.
2. Uncertainty—Federal policy can either increase or de-
    crease uncertainty and thereby have a significant adverse

> or positive effect on investment or other decisions by which
> the economy adjusts. The instability of monetary policy, for
> instance, has introduced an additional amount of uncer-
> tainty into investment markets.
>
> 3.   Lack of Capacity—In low-income neighborhoods, local res-
> idents have been largely left out of the development pro-
> cess which has thwarted the growth of local capacity to deal
> with complex social and economic issues.
>
> 4.   Lack of Coordination—There has been little integration or
> coordination among key parts of the economic or political
> systems; for example, there exists the gap and adversarial
> relationship between the public and private sectors.

These factors may explain why the development process fails in
some regions. Some barriers are public in nature and some private,
but most involve some sort of interaction between the two sectors.

This discussion implies three different policy responses in the
design of economic programs, depending on the diagnosis of the
causes of a development problem. First, if the problem is not serious, if it cannot be solved by public intervention or if the burden of
the problem is borne evenly by a broad section of the community,
then no action should be taken. Second, if the problem is transitional and is borne disproportionately by a narrow section of the
community, and if it does not result from market failure, or if the
cost of correcting the failure exceeds the cost of the failure, then
the response should be to provide compensation. Finally, if the
problem is serious and caused by market failure, and the cost of the
new policy is less than the cost of inaction, then the response should
be to introduce a development program.

We should note that the diagnosis that distinguishes inaction
from compensation is a judgment about the equity aspect of the
distribution of the burden associated with the development problem. A new program is the appropriate response rather than inaction or compensation if the diagnosis determines that the problem
is caused by market failure and that a new program would be cost
effective.

Designing Economic Policy

The purpose of this chapter is to describe the process through
which the public sector can design effective economic policy, not to

define the policy itself. The elements of the strategy will vary according to the types of problems faced and the programs already in place.

Designing a strategy is, essentially, assigning policy to meet the four objectives described earlier. This process can be imagined as being one of filling in the boxes of a matrix. The matrix has a column for each of the objectives: increased macroeconomic growth rate, aiding distressed areas, aiding the disadvantaged, and improving job quality. There is a row in the matrix for each of the eight policy levers: the labor market, land-use planning, development finance, energy policy, taxation, transportation policy, infrastructure development, and regulation.

We cannot, in this chapter, explore each of the matrix entries. To illustrate the process through which state and local governments must proceed as they define their overall strategy, let us briefly examine one "row" from this matrix and show how, by defining the specific objectives and identifying policy options, economic policy makers can determine the shape of a local development strategy. Let us consider development finance policy options and how they meet the four basic development objectives. The options defined are not necessarily effective or appropriate programs, but state and local governments must explore all possible options and then identify those which best meet local needs and which overcome real factor market barriers.

The first possible objective of finance policy is to increase the macroeconomic growth rate. Based on this objective, one goal would be to increase the supply of risk capital. This could be accomplished by reducing the state capital gains tax; by deferring capital gains taxation when gains are reinvested in intrastate business; by abolishing corporate income taxes for the first two years for a new corporation; by setting up a state finance agency for new business-new product development; by directing public pensions to invest a certain percent of their resources in intrastate business start-ups; or by reducing state income tax on interest income earned by savers who deposit in a "state enterprise fund."

A second goal drawn from the object of increasing the macroeconomic growth rate is to increase the supply of debt capital to small businesses. The available options to this goal are requiring all state-chartered banks to invest a certain percent of their assets in small businesses, reducing corporate tax rates for banks on the interest on loans to small businesses, providing state loan guarantees, or encourging the development of a secondary market for the guaranteed portion of loans to small businesses.

Finally, it is possible to raise the macroeconomic growth rate by increasing the availability of funds for research and development (R and D). The three methods of doing this are:

1. Allowing the instant expensing of R and D spending for state tax purposes;
2. Providing state matching grants for R and D investments; and
3. Offering state universities' facilities for R and D activities.

The second objective is the aiding of distressed areas, and the first possible goal of this objective would be to stimulate risk-capital investment in distressed areas. This could be done with any of the above listed programs based on geographic eligibility. Other options include the provision of extra-investment tax credits or grants to investments in distressed areas, the provision of state grants to Small Business Investment Corporations with a distressed area focus, and the development of a high-risk loan loss reserve fund for investments in distressed areas. A second goal could be aiding small businesses in distressed areas by requiring banks to make a certain portion of their loans to businesses in distressed areas, or by targeting state pension fund investments to distressed areas.

The third major objective is aiding the disadvantaged. One possible goal is the stimulation of risk capital for minority entrepeneurs. The possible options to attain this goal are:

1. Providing state grants to Minority Enterprise Small Business Investment Corporations;
2. Providing technical assistance for minority entrepeneur development;
3. Granting loan guarantees for minority businesses;
4. Granting double deduction of losses from income against state corporate income tax for banks for investments in minority business;
5. Targeting loan guarantee programs;
6. Providing premiums to banks for loans to small minority businesses;
7. Developing a high-risk, state loan agency for minority businesses; and

8.   Providing loan subsidies for firms that purchase a large proportion of inputs from minority suppliers.

The final objective is improving job quality. This can be accomplished by improving working conditions by granting tax exempt loans or rapid depreciation for investments in equipment or facilities that improve health, safety, or recreational facilities, or by providing state matching grants for the above investments. Another goal of improved job quality would be to increase options for upward mobility. This could be accomplished by providing low-interest loans or tax credits for firms that provide training to disadvantaged workers or by providing technical assistance to aid firms implementing upward mobility programs. Finally, job quality could be improved by reducing cyclical instability through the provision of both low interest loans for firms with work sharing programs and interest subsidies based upon the countercyclical level of firm inventories.

These options represent only a sample of the possibilities that an imaginative state or local government can develop. The important steps are to define the generic issues within each broad objective and then to explore the powers of the state or city to influence public and private decisions within each of these issues. This exercise necessarily involves many different state or local agencies as well as the tax and budget departments. Policy makers must, therefore, define these issues and then coordinate the efforts of many departments in helping define options. Having defined the options, the task is then to determine their probable effectiveness. This involves evaluating how effectively the program overcomes a genuine market barrier. Too little is known about the nature and extent of market barriers and the effectiveness of alternative programs to determine, on a rigorous basis, which program should be strenuously pursued. We must therefore proceed with caution. As we learn from our experience, we shall be able to recommend measures with more confidence. On that front, we should observe that funding the line operation of a development program, yet not funding the ongoing evaluation of the effectiveness of that program by an unbiased and competent group, will not serve the long-run goals of designing an effective development strategy. Yet evaluation is rarely considered by state and local planners and budget officials. Ultimately, the public sector must learn from program initiatives by financing systematic evaluations of what works and what has failed.

THE ROLE OF PLANNING

The preceding section outlined, very briefly, the iterative process of economic policy development. Each iteration is governed, broadly, by annual budget cycles.[4] We can summarize the steps as:

1. Data gathering and analysis,
2. Identification of economic problems,
3. Diagnosis of causes of problems,
4. Identification of policy options,
5. Evaluation of options, and
6. Selection of appropriate options.

This process does not correspond to traditional planning activity. The conclusion is that planning must shift toward policy analysis. This means that the structure of regional planing agencies must change.

These changes will entail, first , the integration of planning agenices within line-operating agencies including local economic development districts that have successfully moved beyond dependence on EDA funds to build local political and fiscal support, among others. Second, although some funds will be available from state governments for substate planning groups, it is likely to flow only to those groups that have garnered local support. State governments are much more sensitive to local political issues than are federal agencies. Third, planners wil play an increased role in coordinating economic development functions. With severly curtailed institutional support, local success will depend heavily upon the extent to which such disparate organizations as Industrial Development Agencies, Private Industry Councils, Economic Development Districts, Vocational Education Advisory groups, City and County Economic Development Agencies, and Chambers of Commerce can act together.

Finally, planning schools must emphasize more strongly than they do now issues such as public finance, economic analysis, law, development finance, and human resource development. To many, this may seem like a prescription that condemns planning to a wholly reactive role. However, I do not believe this is the case. Planning has played almost no role in state and local economic policy in the past. Only by learning much more detail about the development process can planning contribute to the design of a public strategy. A more direct connection with ongoing programs is the sole way for planners to contribute to specific policy recommendations.

7. Regional Health Care Planning

Jack V. Boyd

INTRODUCTION

The impact of health planning on health status and health services is difficult to measure. This difficulty, coupled with the lack of a supportive constituency, contributed to President Carter's proposal to reduce federal financial participation in the regional health planning program. Withdrawal of all federal financial participation is now proposed by President Reagan's adminstration. A popular subject of discussion in health planning circles concerns how and why support for regional health planning has disintegrated. There are as many viewpoints as there are people involved in health planning programs.

As long as there was optimism, regional health planning was viewed favorably; community leaders were active, needs were agreed upon, and resources were available to fill those needs. As charges for personal health and sickness services claimed ever larger shares of people's income, the responsibility for restraining charges was deposited publicly on the doorstep of the regional health planning program. The tools for restraining charges were not in the hands of either regional or state health planning and development organizations.

81

The short future is not bright for regional health planning. Unregulated competition is presented as a better approach. Renewed awareness that competition ignores equity and that resources are limited will result in the realization that a regional, public interest focused organism is needed to monitor competing claims to scarce resources. At the very least, those who claim resources, whether providers or consumers, must be afforded a publicly visible place to bring their cause or grievance. In the following pages, I will discuss the role of the federal government in the development of regional health planning systems with special reference to the State of Oklahoma.

THE FEDERAL GOVERNMENT AND REGIONAL HEALTH CARE SYSTEMS

A brief review of the past will help clarify why regional health planning finds itself in the present situation. In 1946, the Hill-Burton Program was initiated. Its function was to provide financial assistance to nonprofit and publicly operated hospitals, nursing homes, and clinics. Its aims were to help ensure the availability of services and to plan the development of facilities on a basis that would regionalize specialized services. A small, capable cadre of career public health personnel, the commission corps, ran the U.S. Public Health Service with the Surgeon General in charge. This specialized group worked with state and territorial health officers who, in turn, worked with county, city, and city-county health departments. In its latter stages, the Hill-Burton Program financially assisted local health facilities planning organizations in cities. These committees were usually composed of community financial, medical, and industrial leaders.

It is worth noting that the Department of Health, Education and Welfare (HEW) was created in the early 1950s with Ms. Oveta Culp Hobby as its first secretary. One of the secretary's first determinations was that the provision of federal funds for public health services allocated to state and local health departments were not really necessary. This caused problems in the financing of state and local public health services. In Oklahoma, the response was passage of a constitutional amendment enabling each county to levy and collect taxes on real property for local public health services. This has been done in two-thirds of the counties.

In November 1960, President Eisenhower's Commission on National Goals published a report entitled *Goals for Americans.* Chapter 11 of Part I of the report addresses health in the following words:

The demand for medical care has enormously increased. To meet it we must have more doctors, nurses, and other medical personnel. There should be more hospitals, clinics and nursing homes. Greater effectiveness in the use of such institutions will reduce over-all requirements. There is a heavy responsibility on the medical and public health professions to contribute better solutions (President's Commission on National Goals, 1960).

The report went on to say that "Federal grants for the construction of hospitals should be continued and extended to other medical facilities. Increased private, state and federal support is necessary for training doctors." Finally, it concluded that "further efforts are needed to reduce the burden of the cost of medical care. Extension of medical insurance is necessary, through both public and private agencies." Part III of the Report was titled *Financial Accounting*. It noted that the total spending of federal, state, and local governments was $135 billion or 27 percent of GNP. It further noted that eight percent of GNP, or $36 billion of the $135 billion, represented transfer payments such as social security. The Commission contended that considerable reform of the taxing mechanisms which fund health care and planning was essential to the attainment of national goals. It suggested revision of the federal tax system in order to close loopholes in the structure to ensure equity in the provision of health services, and to encourage savings which it considered vital to economic expansion. The Commission suggested that

Many state governments must find new tax sources. Local governments must be freed of unnecessary restriction on taxing and borrowing powers, and the pronounced inequalities in the property tax bases of local jurisdictions should be corrected.

The goals presented in 1960 became an agenda for action during the following decade. The national health agenda was indeed substantial. In no particular order, it included the community mental health center act, the development disabilities program, Medicare for the elderly, Medicaid for the medically indigent, community health centers, regional medical programs to extend knowledge and skills in heart, cancer, stroke, and kidney disease service, et cetera. Many of these programs specified population criteria for geographic area jurisdictions. In Oklahoma, most of these were accommodated within the five geographic regions established by the Hill-Burton Council.

The report of the National Commission on Community Health, *Health is a Community Affair,* was published in 1966. Its sources were documents from organized studies of health needs in 21 communities and the locally developed plans for dealing with them. The principal conclusions were:

1. That often health problems cannot be effectively solved if activities are confined to city limits, to county or parish lines, or in some instances, to state boundaries. The organization and delivery of community health services must be based on the "Community of Solution."
2. All communities must take the action necessary to provide comprehensive health services to all people in each community.
3. That people within communities must be knowledgeable about health services and practice good health habits.
4. Environmental contamination must be controlled.

It was of the utmost importance that this national commission saw health planning as a regional problem and suggested a regional solution.

The National Health Planning Act (P.L. 89-749) was enacted in 1967-68. It provided block grants for public health purposes, project grants to develop needed health services, funding for substate health planning organizations, and funding for State Health Planning Agencies. It was strongly supported by the Association of State and Territorial Health Officers, whose president was Oklahoma's Commissioner of Health. This Act was to initiate community planned approaches to the implementation and operation of public health services and to broaden public health's role. It became law after Medicare, Medicaid, Office of Economic Opportunity (OEO), and other public programs to remove economic barriers from access to medical care for at-risk populations had been enacted.

In the meantime, other Departments of the U.S. Government initiated programs which required substate planning entities. It seemed that each federal agency or program desired a specific presence in the office of every governor and every mayor, in addition to ties to a specified operating agency within the state or local governments. Trying to deal with the varying requirements was vexing to anyone who recognized that there cannot be coordinated effort without a superior power. When the superior power was not singular, but multiple, new kinds of organizations were developed. The Office of Management and Budget (OMB) had a notable role in extending the federal presence. OMB established the A-95 Review Process which required a system of state and substate clearinghouses to review and report on the worthiness and potential for duplication of proposed local and state projects using certain federal funds.

The Department of Housing and Urban Development (HUD) was the federal agency which disbursed the greatest amount of new money in the West South Central regional of the country. HUD required that a state be divided into standard planning areas. Since there appeared no rational way to do this, it was done through the political process. After holding several public hearings, the Governor of Oklahoma delineated 11 Standard Planning Areas (SPA s). Councils of government were then organized in each of these SPA s. The councils of government were chartered as nonprofit corporations. Membership was restricted to county commissioners, city council members, and mayors, all of whom represented general purpose governments. Soil Conservation Districts (SCD s) and chambers of commerce were initially included, while local boards of education and county boards of health were not included. Subsequently, the SCD s and chambers of commerce were excluded as being inappropriate. The councils of government were financed in part by dues from members, but principally by federal grants for the sponsorship or performance of various functions.

Health planning, under the model promoted by *Health is a Community Affair* retained the state government as the pivotal power in the planning arrangement. There was no rigid prescription of health plan content or arrangement. With the knowledge that the Comprehensive Health Planning Act (P.L. 89-749) proceeded from the theory that health is a community-based issue, Oklahoma endeavored to foster community choice in the organization and sponsorship of the 11 SPA health planning organizations. These organizations were referred to as 314-B Agencies. In the Tulsa and Oklahoma City SPAs, Oklahoma's major metropolitan areas, private nonprofit corporations were organized for health planning purposes. The State Health Planning Agency involved itself directly in forging relationships between these nonprofit health planning corporations and the councils of government. This arrangement worked quite well in the Tulsa area, which had an existing intergovernmental metropolitan planning commission that had functioned effectively in physical planning for at least two decades. The remaining nine SPAs had small populations living in large, sparsely populated geographic areas. Only one had a city of more than 100,000; two had cities of more than 60,000; five had cities of nearly 20,000; and two had cities of less than 10,000.

Oklahoma's State Health Planning Agency was located at one time or another in the State Health Department, the State Office of Finance, and the State Office of Economic and Community Affairs. At present it is a free-standing, statutory five-member commission of the state government. There were certain advantages and certain disadvantages to each location. In appears now that the commission was the best overall arrangement.

The state endeavored to develop and maintain collegial relationships with the substate health planning agencies. Some of the multipurpose, multijurisdictional sponsors of health planning in the nine SPAs were prone to claim excessive indirect overheads, and therefore, it was necessary for the state to ensure that resources allocated for health planning were used for health planning purposes. As planning did not directly control implementation funds, the state's role was to acknowledge and give voice to needs and to provide technical assistance and public visibility to the resources required to meet these needs. It could also identify apparent surpluses both publicly and, more directly, to persons providing financial support to them. There were difficulties with hospital capacities, especially in suburban areas. As people and sickness care manpower exited central cities and relocated in adjacent suburban areas, the pressure for facilities increased. This is a phenomenon that has occurred in most Standard Metropolitan Statistical Districts (SMSAs) in the Sunbelt states.

For the most part, 314-B Area Health Planning Councils were able to recruit and retain the participation of a broad base of community, health, business, political, academic, and voluntary sector leaders. Some community leaders began to pull back from participation following implementation of the review of proposed facilities. The 314-B agencies had no direct powers of enforcement and derived their influence from making the public aware of proposals and the 314-B agency recommendations. Regulatory review participation was further formalized through 314-B agency involvement in the Section 1122 Review Programs.

In other ways, the state's position as a pivotal power became somewhat tenuous as some councils of government moved to use their review and comment functions under the OMB Clearinghouse requirements to leverage operating programs of state government. This course led to some conflict between governors and councils of government. It also led to conflicts between central cities in SMSAs and other smaller municipal members of the councils.

The move toward what became the National Health Planning and Resources Development Act began as substate planning organizations, encouraged by the national level sponsors, searched for increased powers and, as the participants in their health planning components desired increased clout. Congressmen Roy of Kansas and Hastings of New York were the principal proponents. At the time there was an expectation that National Health Insurance was about to become reality, and there was an intent to have organized substate planning and development organizations in place. P.L. 93-641, the National Health Planning and Resources Development Act of 1974 became law in January 1975. The act was regulatory in nature. It removed the states from their position of pivotal power and placed in that position the Secretary of HEW.

One of the first requirements of the act was the division of the nation into Health Service Areas consisting generally of SMSAs and populations of 500,000 to 3,000,000 people. Some latitude was provided in the criteria. Responsibility for proposing Health Service Areas for substate planning and development purposes reposed with the governors. There was some flexibility for trade offs among governors of contiguous states. Each governor recommended Health Service Area configurations, and the Secretary of HEW had the power to accept or reject them. Within each Health Service Area there was to be a Health Systems Agency (HSA). Ultimately, there were 212 HSAs. Most of them were free-standing, nonprofit corporations. In Oklahoma, the governor recommended that the entire state be an HSA.

Membership on HSA boards was specified to be representative of the characteristics of the general population residing in each area. A consumer majority was required. Lengths of terms were three years with no more than two succcessive terms for an individual. Composition of these boards did not reflect the mix of leadership found on the boards of the 314-B agencies. Over time, aided by stringent regulations, the HSAs began to acquire the image of regulatory agencies. Developmental funds were never allocated, and national health insurance did not come to be.

THE FUTURE OF REGIONAL HEALTH PLANNING

The principal health concern of people appears to be the ever increasing cost of health care. A hospital confinement is quite expensive. The costs of nursing home care and other long-term care arrangements are also costly. The future of health planning lies, at least for the short-term, with state governments. The Congress has amended P.L. 93-641, as amended by the Omnibus Reconciliation Act of 1981, in ways that enable the governor of each state to assume the full health planning function by notification to the Secretary of Health and Human Services. Higher expenditure thresholds and exemptions for proposed new health services have also been provided in the amendments. Certificate of Need Programs are mandated by state statutes. The next sessions of the various state legislatures will, hopefully, bring some focus to the matter of organized health planning programs.

8. Regional Transportation Finance

Richard S. Page

INTRODUCTION

Regional transportation finance has emerged over the past 20 years as a key issue of public policy. In 1961, Congress authorized the first specific federal assistance for planning for mass transit. Section 310(B) of the Housing Act of 1961 states the purpose to be

> To assist State and local governments in solving planning problems resulting from the increasing concentration of population in metropolitan and other urban areas, including smaller communities; to facilitate comprehensive planning for urban development, including coordinated transportation systems, on a continuing basis by such governments; and to encourage such governments to establish and improve planning staffs . . . .

The following year Congress stipulated in the Highway Act that transportation planning was to be conducted on a regional basis and was to consist of the three "C's"—it was to be comprehensive, cooperative, and continuing (1962 Highway Act).

89

This "three-C" transportation planning was to be conducted by metropolitan or regional agencies or boards, sometimes part of councils of government and sometimes not. Planning funds, as well as influence and control, came from state highway departments. In many urban areas, this process simply provided better planning methods for more highway facilities, which could be constructed and operated largely by federal, state, and local gas taxes. Federal law, state and local laws, and even state constitutions restricted gas · tax revenues for highway projects and a small portion of the restricted funds were earmarked for regional transportation, i.e., highway planning. The planning was, consequently, not very comprehensive or cooperative even if continuing.

Today this system is generally still in effect. Transportation planning is required by federal law to be conducted on a regional basis but is dominated by highway needs and funds. It is performed by councils of government or transportation planning boards, funded by federal and state gas taxes and supervised and heavily influenced by state highway departments which are now called transportation departments. The planning and financing of regional or metropolitan transit programs has evolved separately because the highway-dominated planning process did not properly emphasize urban mass transit facilities. As a consequence, separate federal legislation developed to promote urban mass transportation programs.

Thus, regional transportation finance has developed as a key issue of public policy with two dimensions: planning and financing of highway facilities, and planning and financing of transit facilities. To some extent, they merge in the generalized planning provided by councils of government and in the construction of joint facilities such as exclusive busways or rapid transit lines in freeway medians. To some extent, they directly compete, such as when urban area policymakers have chosen to withdraw interstate highway segments and substitute mass transit projects. This has happened pursuant to the 1973 Highway Act in several areas, such as Boston, New York, Philadelphia, Washington, Chicago, and Portland.

The emergence of the councils of government has also raised some interesting questions of public policy. Should voluntary organizations such as these perform regional transportation planning? Should the regional transportation planning responsibility be divorced from the financial decision-making process? Is this a stop-gap or interim measure to resolve regional problems or a lasting solution to our regional problems? The achievements of these voluntary organizations have been mixed. In any event, they serve a valuable function as a conference or forum for local elected officials. Councils of government, however, are not agencies which operate or construct highway or transit programs.

The sponsoring and operating agencies for urban highway and transit programs are different, their governing officials are different, the source and ratio of funds are different, and the methods and politics of finance are different. Their history is also different. Highways have been regarded as a governmental responsibility since at least 1921 when the Federal Bureau of Public Roads was established. It was not until 1965 that a separate federal agency for mass transportation was formed. More to the point, in almost all American cities, transit facilities and services were provided and financed by private companies until the late 1960s and early 1970s.

The emergence and growth of regional transit authorities to plan, finance, construct, and operate public transportation services has occurred suddenly, between approximately 1965 and 1975. It can be attributed to three interwoven factors: urban areas expanded in population and geographical size requiring the development of new, more widely based organizations to manage services needed by both central cities and suburbs; privately owned companies encountered business difficulties and, as they went bankrupt, prompted governmental action to create successor public organizations; and federal aid became available for transit planning, then for acquisiton of private assets and public construction, and in 1974, for operating assistance. This sudden emergence of public transit authorities and the issues of regional transportation finance they pose are the focus of this paper.

THE EVOLUTION OF REGIONAL TRANSPORTATION AUTHORITIES

In 1964, Congress enacted the basic and important Urban Mass Transportation Act (UMTA). It greatly expanded the federal interest in mass transit and the scope of federal aid to include not just planning, but the acquisiton of private companies, the purchase of rolling stock, rehabilitation of old facilities, and the design and construction of new facilities, including garages, rail lines, stations, and related developments.

This act was amended and broadened in 1968, 1970, 1974, and 1978. The 1970 changes dramatically increased the federal authorization, and the 1974 amendments authorized federal aid for operating and maintenance expenses in addition to capital. In 1978, the law was amended to provide federal aid to small urban and rural areas. A major transit bill passed both Houses of Congress in the fall of 1980 but was stopped in the Senate after the November elections.

These repeated Congressional enactments plus steadily larger annual appropriations and the stewardship of the urban mass transportation program by four presidential administrations expanded the budget, scope, impact, and success of the program. After 15 years, from Fiscal 1965 to Fiscal 1980, federal capital grants to urban mass transportation total about $15.2 billion. Federal aid plus matching state and local funds have purchased 43,370 new buses, paid for 3,218 rapid transit cars and 497 light rail cars, rebuilt 56 miles of rail, financed 240 miles of new urban subway in cities and metropolitan areas across the country. New subway systems have been started in Atlanta, Baltimore, Miami, and Buffalo. San Francisco's Bay Area Rapid Transit (BART) and Washington's Metro were started and financed separately from the regular UMTA program.

Despite these significant advances in federal transit assistance, it must be noted that several old biases still remain. Federal funds for urban highways are given on a 90-10 matching basis. For urban transit facilities, the ratio is 80-20. The Federal Department of Transportation requires an "Alternatives Analysis" process to justify new rail transit programs on any "major capital investment" over $100 million. No such justification is needed for new highways.

The small federal program of operating aid, begun in 1974, doubled in size in four years to $1.1 billion allocated to 279 urbanized areas by federal formula. More importantly, it has become a primary source of revenue for many small and medium-sized transit agencies, providing as much as 50 percent of total revenue to some. On the transit industry balance sheet for 1979, the national revenue column showed 46.1 percent of revenues from fares, 15.7 percent from federal operating assistance, 11.1 percent from state operating assistance, 24.5 percent from local operating assistance, and 2.6 percent from miscellaneous sources. The expense side showed 48.7 percent for direct transportation costs, 26.1 percent for maintenance including fuel, 18.3 percent for general administration, and 6.9 percent for a range of miscellaneous activities.[1] In 1979, fares as a percent of costs ranged from 26 percent in San Antonio to over 58 percent in New York.

As the federal program grew in size and scope, so did the role of state agencies and funds, and the number and size of regional transportation authorities. In the early 1960s, the number of publicly owned municipal transit organizations was less than a dozen, including New York, Boston, Chicago, and Seattle. In fact, each of these four municipally owned and operated mass transit systems were reorganized during this same period into new regional or metropolitan agencies. In all four cases, state legislation provided the reorganization, and the new transit authorities in Boston and New York became state agencies. Dedicated funding was provided on a metropolitan basis in Seattle and Chicago as part of the reorganization. Today there are approximately 350 publicly owned transit authorities in the 279 urbanized areas. There are, in addition, another 336 private companies offering regularly scheduled, fixed route transit service, but by far the bulk of the vehicles, routes, ridership, services, and costs are provided by the publicly owned entities (U.S. Department of Transportation, 1981). Some are municipal in ownership, management, and scope of service. Some are publicly owned but contract with private operators. Most are separately established by state law or city or metropolitan referendum, and organized as independent governmental authorities. Some of these have their own dedicated source of funds; some have just recently acquired such a source; most depend on annual general fund appropriations from state and local governments. All struggle every year to find the proper mix of service, fares, and operating assistance.

The result is an unusual, complex, and tenuous partnership of governments and financial arrangements. This partnership responds to the rapid growth of transit needs and service over the past 15 years, following two decades of transit neglect and decline after World War II.

The rapid expansion of transit service, organizations, funding and complex intergovernmental relationships, coupled with the philosophies of the Reagan Administration and a more conservative Congress have suddenly caused a slowing down and reexamination of all these issues, especially the federal role. That rethinking is no doubt necessary and healthy, provided it does not turn into another period of stagnation, neglect, and decline of public transportation services when the nation can ill afford to reduce mobility or become more dependent on the automobile.

Space does not permit reciting the circumstances in each city of the decline of privately owned transit, the emergence of a public transit authority, the role of federal planning, capital, and operating aid, and the continuing struggle for funds from public sources to pay for a growing public service. The pattern across the nation is clear. New public authorities popped up with increasing frequency in the late 1960s and early 1970s. As late as 1972, private transit owner-operators in Los Angeles, Cleveland, and Washington were surviving and paying costs from fares, only to give way suddenly to public agencies and public funds. Special legislation was rushed through Maryland, Washington, D.C., Virginia, and the Congress in 1973 to enable the Washington Metropolitan Area Transit Authority (WMATA) to acquire four failing private companies and create one regional publicly owned and operated bus system. Atlanta held a state-authorized referendum in 1972 to create a metropolitan transit authority serving the central city and three counties and to levy a one cent sales tax throughout that area to pay for building and operating a new subway and an improved bus system. Denver and Seattle both reorganized and created new metropolitan agencies in 1972.

Successful transit referenda creating new authorities and levying new taxes subsequently occurred in Chicago (1975), Cleveland (1977), San Antonio (1977), and Houston (1978). New publicly owned and supported transit programs emerged, usually through new regional transit authorities, in Pittsburgh, Miami, Philadelphia, Baltimore, Minneapolis, St. Louis, San Francisco, Portland, Detroit, San Diego, and most big and medium-sized cities. Some had special taxes; some did not.

Taxes for transit purposes have been levied on sales in Denver, Atlanta, Los Angeles, Seattle, Cleveland, Houston, New York, on motor vehicles in Seattle, on payrolls in Portland and Cincinnati, on gross receipts in New York and San Francisco, on professions and businesses, et cetera. Only a very few urban areas rely on dedicated gas taxes. Among these are the City of Detroit, the Chicago metropolitan region, and northern Virginia. In the case of northern Virginia, about one-third of its operating assistance to WMATA is covered by gas taxes. Many of the largest metropolitan areas which depend heavily on mass transit lack any dedicated or assured funding. They engage in "pass-the-hat" budgets which cause continuing, difficult political struggles in these big urban centers. Boston, for example, has an advisory council of 78 cities and towns, including the City of Boston, which tries to agree on the annual transit budget and municipal assessments. New York, until June 1981, relied on state, New York City, and suburban general fund contributions to provide the operating assistance and the local match for capital grants amounting to a 1980 level of over $600 million in nonfederal aid. Philadelphia established a new regional transit authority in 1964 but failed to provide any dedicated or assigned revenue. The regional transit authority was left helplessly dependent on annual appropriations from the state and local communities in the region. Pittsburgh, Washington, Miami, St. Louis, Minneapolis, and Detroit are other large urban regions with no dedicated transit taxes. In Los Angeles, a tax on sales levied by the state falls far short of meeting the city's transit operating and capital needs.

Despite these financial problems, most of these metropolitan areas have forged ahead over the last decade to improve and expand transit service. The money has somehow been found, through a combination of state and local sources, with many states developing during the 1970s mass transportation agencies and funding sources to assist localities, large and small, and rural areas in their states. Transit service has been expanded, new equipment has been purchased, labor rates have gone up steadily from extremely depressed levels, and now diesel fuel costs have doubled and doubled again since 1973, putting new pressure on transit operating costs.

The basic fact of the past 15 years has been the conversion of transit from the private sector to the public. If the farebox alone covered operating costs for private operators as late as 1972, it is abundantly clear that now transit is a public service in big urban centers, middle-sized cities, and rural areas throughout the world as well as America. As a public service, transit has rather suddenly enjoyed government grants and subsidies as an alternative to bankrupt or subsidized private companies, but has also become enmeshed in governmental controls, regulations and red tape of many varieties, legislative and executive struggles, metropolitan politics, and citizen participation.

In the past year, the debate has sharpened over the role of fares (user fees) to pay for transit service. Public policy since the 1964 Act has been to stabilize fares in order to attract riders. In Seattle, Atlanta, Denver, Chicago, Houston and other areas, a principal reason for the transit tax referendum was to provide government operating assistance so the fare did not have to rise or rise as much. This policy has been eminently successful; ridership has increased 23 percent just since 1973. In some cities, annual gains of 20 percent or more have been recorded.

Now, however, since 1979, as double-digit inflation affected transit costs and the reality of generous wage settlements occurred, fares have been forced to rise, and we have witnessed a subsequent levelling off of ridership. Boards of directors, local elected officials, state legislators, and even federal officials have moved to raise fares sharply to 90 cents in Chicago, one dollar in Miami, 75 cents for each bus and subway ride in New York with no transfer between them, et cetera. Fare increases have been sudden, big, and repetitive in the past 24 months and are having an adverse effect on ridership.

TRANSPORTATION: A REGIONAL POLICY ISSUE

Given the rapid evolution of new regional transit authorities and the emphasis on transit as a public service, these arguments over organization, planning, and finance will certainly continue. In my judgment, regional transit authorities must continue to exist as the necessary instrument for political decision making and for management of primary transit services and facilities for a metropolitan region.

Generally, decisions should be made at the lowest level of government, but that level of government must have both the responsibility and authority to implement its functional programs. There are many activities which can be terminated at political boundaries so that the quality and quantity of service can and should be determined by that political entity commensurate with its priorities and fiscal capacity. If some sort of parity or equity among several small units of government is desired, financial assistance should be forthcoming from a larger political unit. However, those functional activities which directly impact contiguous jurisdictions and which cannot be managed in isolation must be governed by a consortium of political units. In most of our large metropolitan areas, public transportation fits that definition.

A public transportation system impacts where people live and where they work. It expands the employment base of an area by providing access throughout. It provides an alternative and makes available valuable urban land for uses other than parking facilities. It provides a tool whereby master plans can be formulated and implemented and the region can develop according to its desires. In the case of a regional public transportation system, the sum of the parts do not equal the whole. Several small, separate and individual transit systems will not be as effective or as cost-productive as when integrated into a regional unit. Duplication of maintenance and storage facilities can be avoided; through-routing can be developed so as to minimize the need for passenger transfers; and economies of scale can be realized through the use of more efficient types of equipment. And political decisions affecting a metropolitan area can be hammered out in a regionally based organization.

The desirability and functions of a regional organization do not require that it be the sole provider of urban mass transit service. Other methods of ride-sharing are working and can be expected to expand, given the cumbersomeness of large agencies and the high costs of transit union labor protected by federal law and regulation. Other methods include private and government-sponsored vanpools and carpools, subscription and contract bus service, and localized government-aided bus service such as Montgomery County's Ride-On program in the Washington metropolitan area. These other methods also contribute to the diversity of urban mass transit and the complexity of decision making on the level of service and the allocation of public funds.

THE FAIR-FARE DECISION

This last issue of allocating public funds has many aspects. To what extent should a public transit system be self-supporting? What criteria should be used in structuring the fare system? Should fares be kept low so as to assist the lower-income residents? What, if any, supplemental revenue sources should be used in conjunction with farebox revenues? Should individual areas of service be measured only in terms of cost-effectiveness? What level of transportation can a region afford? How is service and the cost of it equated between the center city and suburbs?

   As an illustration, a brief description of financing and fare decision issues in the Washington area might be helpful. Fares cover almost 50 percent of WMATA's bus and rail operating costs. This means that the users of the system are paying one-half of the operating costs while the other half is being subsidized by nonusers. This is a controversial and unresolved issue in Washington and around the country. Generally, the District of Columbia advocates a low fare approach which necessitates higher governmental payments from the eight local jurisdictions and two states participating in WMATA. The five Virginia jurisdictions usually press for higher fares and lower subsidies while the two Maryland counties fall somewhere in between these two philosophies. The Board of Directors sets the fares but in policy and practice adopts what Maryland, Virginia, and District officials want in those three main jurisdictions. The differing approaches to this issue have led to the Washington Metro's bus system having one of the most complicated and confusing fare systems in the world. Metro has different fares for different periods of the day. There are flat fares within some jurisdictions and zone fares within others, and Metro has special discounts for the elderly and disabled and different discounts for students. In some cases, it allows free transfers from the rail system to the bus system; in other cases, it charges for the transfer. On the other hand, there is never a transfer privilege for a bus to rail trip. Metro has seven types of two-week passes which vary in the discount provided. It also has tokens and tickets, and considerable criticism and public confusion.

   The complexity of the fare system is related to the necessity to allocate deficits among the participating jurisdictions. Since bus service can be operated regionally but the level of service can vary by jurisdiction, bus deficits are allocated on what is called a cost-revenue formula. Costs incurred within an individual jurisdiction minus revenues generated within that jurisdiction equals the subsidy of that jurisdiction. This allows a great deal of local option over service and fare levels but leads to a confusing state of affairs for the users of the system.

   On the other hand, Metrorail has to be operated on a regional basis and service and fares have to be uniform. Train schedules and train consists cannot be altered at political boundaries, nor can equipment be developed which would accommodate several different fare structures. Consequently, there are uniform levels of fares and service and allocate subsidy requirements based upon a three-factor formula:

1. Relative urbanized population within each jurisdiction as a measure of community benefits;
2. Relative ridership by residents of each jurisdiction as a measure of user benefits; and
3. Relative number of operable stations in each jurisdiction as a measure of potential economic benefits.

To date, the rail fare structure and allocation process have been fairly well accepted. However, as the rail system expands, increasing disagreement is evident between the close-in and outlying jurisdictions over the relative fares to be charged for short versus long trips. It is becoming more and more difficult to find the political compromises for maintaining a uniform rail fare structure.

The fare issue is not simple. Fares are relatively high in Washington, and the complaint is often heard that fares cannot or should not be increased because low-income people will not be able to afford public transportation. The latest evidence in Washington and elsewhere is that higher fares are hurting ridership. I believe that fares are going up too fast and too often. The Board of Directors adopted in October 1981, a third substantial fare increase within 17 months. However, I do not subscribe to the concept that the fare system must be commensurate with the ability of the lower income people to afford it. Transportation systems should not be used as a tool to redistribute income. The establishment of a low-fare system subsidizes the wealthy more than the poor. If the poor need to be assisted to use transit, a program of transit stamps administered by local governments would be an effective and equitable method of achieving this goal.

Some advocate a fare structure based upon the ability to pay. Others argue that there should be a fare-cost relationship; the more it costs to provide the trip, the higher the fare should be. Still others advocate that fares be correlated with benefits; the longer the trip is, the higher the fare should be. This distance-based fare is in effect in the Washington area and elsewhere, but not in New York or Toronto. Its disadvantages are confusion to the rider and higher costs of fare collection. The issue will continue to be debated hotly by transit authority directors.

CONCLUSION

Today, after a decade and a half, public transit is firmly established as a governmental service. It cannot, will not, and should not be self-supporting. There are innumerable community or nonuser benefits which justify community financial participation. Cleaner air, energy conservation, decreased street and highway congestion, better utilization of land and increased tax revenues, and implementation of coordinated and planned growth policies are a few of these benefits. While the exact ratio of farebox revenues to costs is difficult to pinpoint and will differ from system to system, I believe it should range between 40 and 60 percent.

If regional transportation systems are not self-supporting, the question then becomes how should they be financed. There is no consistent or pat answer to this question, and the mechanism and the tax source will vary from system to system. However, the evidence of the past decade is that a dedicated tax source must be used to supplement farebox revenues, and that where such dedicated sources are in place, such as in Atlanta, Portland and Seattle, transit programs have prospered and have enhanced those metropolitan areas. The need for dedicated sources will be even more compelling if Congress concurs with the Reagan Administration's plans to eliminate the $1.1 billion of federal operating assistance by Fiscal 1985. Without these dedicated sources, fares must rise even more sharply, or much service will be eliminated, or both. As we study the issues involved in regional transportation finance, with special emphasis on mass transit service, the need for both the function and the financing is clear. The solutions are not as readily apparent.

PART FOUR

Case Studies

9. Metropolitan Reorganization in the Minneapolis-St. Paul Region

Ted Kolderie

INTRODUCTION

The State of Minnesota has a population of four million people, a mere two percent of the nation as a whole. Nevertheless, it is the source of business enterprises, sociopolitical ideas and institutions, and presidential candidates which far surpass those of many states much larger. To a great extent, these contributions are due to the success of the Twin Cities metropolitan region which, with two million people, represents half of the state population and is 20 times as large as Minnesota's second-ranking urban area, Duluth. The Twin Cities act as the heart and mind of the state by serving as the home to the state capital, to the headquarters of large corporations, to a combined state and land-grant university, and to many trade associations and cultural institutions. The economic, social, and political health of this urban region is what makes Minnesota a significant factor in national affairs. Thus, a threat to this health is a threat to Minnesota as a whole.

The legislature of Minnesota recognized the importance of the Twin Cities by intervening massively in the years between 1967 and 1976 in order to ensure that the forces of urban growth did not put parts of the region at war with each other, as had occurred in so many metropolitan areas. Intervention was also intended to unite the region in such a way as to increase its effectiveness in its competition with the other metropolitan areas around the country. The legislature did this essentially by inserting into the governmental structure of the region a new, metropolitan level which acted essentially as a mechanism for policy leadership and coordination, and also took central control of the finances of the region. It was perhaps the most far-reaching reorganization carried out for any major urban region, and one which David Walker of the Advisory Commission on Intergovernmental Relations (ACIR) later called "Minnesota's major contribution to governmental theory in this country."[1]

This reorganization is now well into its second decade. Completed in terms of the development of its structure and the delineation of its jurisdictional powers in 1976, it settled rapidly into maturity. It is today neither growing institutionally nor is it particularly aggressive on issues of regional policy, but it has held its position as the wave of metropolitan reform has receded nationally. The limited political unification has proved to be strategically highly important for Minnesota and the Metropolitan Council, the governing body, has executed it effectively. The Twin Cities area is today one of the most successful and most widely admired urban regions in America.

Any study of regionalism in the Twin Cities should begin with the essential principles on which this new system of regional governance was constructed. First, the enabling authority came from state legislation rather than local action. The impetus for the legislation came not just at the urging and with the support of people within the region, but also emphatically from the state because of its own larger interest. One important result is that, in contrast to those metropolitan reorganizations that derive their authority from referenda within the region, the basic charter controlling the structure and powers of the metropolitan agencies here is continually open to amendment as new problems arise and changes are needed. The state, refusing to delegate sovereignty, remains responsible if not for the decisions themselves, then for the system that makes the decisions (Harrigan and Johnson, 1978, p.146).

The second principle is that the system was built for the purpose of making policy and political decisions rather than for the operation and administration of programs. There are two dimensions to this central design concept. One is that the policy body, the Metropolitan Council, stands on its own political base; its membership is not interlocked with other levels of local government. The idea of a Council of Governments (COG) was considered, and rejected in 1966-67. These work on questions where interests coincide. Minnesota, however, set out deliberately to build a mechanism able to handle the tough questions on which interests conflict. Municipalities, counties, and schools may, and frequently do, organize regionally to express to the council the interests of local governments. The council, which has some former local officials as well as some former state legislators among its membership, gives these expressions a weight that the importance of local government and its political influence deserve. But, fundamentally, the public interest is not simply the local government interest.

The other dimension of the central design concept is that the Metropolitan Council is itself a nonoperating body. The problem perceived in 1966-67 was not a problem with the competence of either the local units or of the then existing metropolitan special districts. Rather, most agreed that it was a problem of policy coordination. The job of the council was to give early, clear direction to others who will then implement the regional policy. It is the equivalent of the combined function of client, architect, and general contractor on a major building project who gives the direction to the mechanical, electrical, structural and other subcontractors who actually do the work. The importance of this decision became fully clear only after some years, as the concept of "things of metropolitan significance" emerged. The Metropolitan Council, having been denied authority to control all of the decisions of metropolitan public agencies, was given authority over the decisions of local public and even private agencies when these involved an issue critical to metropolitan development. The legislature's decision to set up regional operations, such as sewers, transit, and airports, in separate subordinate regional commissions reduced the scope of the council's ownership. However, through this concept of coordination, the reduction in scope of ownership was more than offset by an expansion of the council's range of control. The central effort was to force the council and its members and staff away from the morass of operational detail, however interesting and controver-

sial, and toward the major policy issues. This requires early
proposals rather than final authority to be effective.

This is an arrangement that works on the principle of decentralization from state to metropolitan region, from Metropolitan
Council outward to regional commissions and downward to local
units. The principles are identical, it was discovered later, with the
management philosophy worked out in such a totally different context as General Motors Corporation.

> Good management rests on a reconciliation of centralization
> and decentralization; or decentralization with coordinated
> control . . . . It was clearly advisable to give each division a
> strong management which would be primarily responsible
> for its business. (But) without adequate control from the cen-
> tral office the divisions got out of hand . . . .The right combi-
> nation of freedom for the divisions and control over them
> could not be set once and for all . . . .Continuing adjustments
> in the relative responsibility are permitted by the decentral-
> ized organization.
>
> The role of the division managers is to make almost all of
> the operating decisions; subject, however, to some important
> qualifications. Their decisions must be consistent with the
> corporation's general policies; the results of the division's
> operations must be reported to the central management; and
> the division managers must 'sell' central management on any
> substantial changes in operating policies and must be open to
> suggestions from the general officers.
>
> This practice of selling major proposals is an important fea-
> ture of our management. Any proposal must be sold to cen-
> tral management; and, if it affects other divisions, it must be
> sold to them as well. Sound management also requires that
> the central office should in most cases sell its proposals to the
> divisions. Our 'selling' approach assures that any basic deci-
> sion is made only after thorough consideration by all parties
> concerned. Our tradition of selling ideas, rather than simply
> giving orders, imposes the need upon all levels of manage-
> ment to make a good case for what they propose (Sloan,
> 1973).

THE ORGANIZATIONAL ARRANGEMENT

The metropolitan area consists of seven counties surrounding the central cities of Minneapolis and St. Paul, about 3000 square miles. The Metropolitan Council, originally 14 districts built on the State Senate districts, is now 16 separately drawn districts; this was done in anticipation of a change to direct-election which did not occur. Members are appointed by the governor after consultation with the legislators representing each council district. Additionally, there is informal input from local officials, from private groups, and, except where a new governor is involved, from the chairman of the Metropolitan Council. Each appointed member serves a four-year term. The chairman is also appointed by the governor for an indefinite term and serves at-large. The chairman, with a full-time paid position, is the key person in a chairman and chief executive officer system. There may also be an executive director. The separate position of planning director disappeared in the time of the second chairman and has not been recreated.

The council appoints the members of most of the regional commissions and, in varying degrees, reviews and controls their plans and their finances. Some are located in downtown St. Paul with the council; some are not.

The staff of the council, presently being cut back, numbers about 200. Its budget, before the cutbacks, had reached about $9,000,000; of that, about $3,500,000 came from federal grants, and about $4,200,000 from the regional property tax of about one-quarter mill and from interest. The council also received about $1,000,000 from charge-backs to the regional commissions.

FUNCTIONAL AREAS

It is more helpful to look at what the Metropolitan Council has done than to look at what it is in terms of formal structure and authority.

Transportation.

The major policy decision by the council in 1972 was not to get into fixed-guideway transit in this region. This required the council to veto a proposal by the Metropolitan Transit Commission (MTC), and provoked an intense conflict with the MTC which continued throughout the 1970s, until, under a new governor and a new

MTC chairman, that agency settled down to its job of running the bus system. Outside observers who believe the ultimate form of transit in any city must be a fixed-guideway system often tend to describe the Twin Cities area as "unable to make a decision." In truth, however, an effective decision has been made in favor of a lower-capital, more flexible system of vehicles not fixed to guideways. There is, in fact, a broader definition of transit in use here, which looks at transit as riding rather than driving alone. Such shared-ride systems as taxis, vanpools, and carpools become a part of the implementation strategy (U.S. Office of Technology Assessment, 1976). The Twin Cities area has become a national leader in the design and development of these low-capital systems. Some reserved right-of-ways for buses and high-occupancy vehicles will soon be under construction. On some freeways these vehicles are given preference to the main line at separate access ramps. There is still flirtation with a light-rail corridor, and the city of St. Paul, for a time, seriously tried for a circulator within its central area. In the present retrenchment, the bus system may withdraw from the outer suburbs, being replaced by paratransit systems both for central city commuting and for local area trips.

Waste.

It was the inability to get agreement on a comprehensive waste treatment and disposal policy in four consecutive sessions in the state legislature, from 1961 to 1967, that directly led to the creation of the Metropolitan Council. In 1969, the council achieved its first great success by securing local agreement, thus enabling legislative action. The result was that small waste-treatment plants discharging to lakes and streams were closed. A huge expansion of the central, downstream treatment plant was begun along with the development of several regional plants. Interceptor capacity was, if anything, overexpanded. More recently, the emphasis has been on solid waste. The decision was made in 1969 to proceed with landfills rather than with incinerators, and the open-burning dumps were closed. And in 1975 the council vetoed a proposal from the Waste Control Commission to build a pyrolosis plant to dispose of sludge from its major treatment plant. The council is now in the final stages of deciding on a site for the disposal of this sludge and ash. The counties are responsible for landfills for the general refuse of the region and—given the political resistance both from landowners and from environmentalists—are promoting incinerators (resource recovery). The council is presently supporting this change, yet the final decision is uncertain. Hazardous waste has recently been made the responsibility of a new state board; its siting process is now nearing completion.

Open Space.

In 1973 the counties intervened to prevent creation of a system in which the regional parks would be owned by a metropolitan commission. The arrangement is now one of metropolitan planning and financing for acquisition and development, with county ownership, operation, and operational-financing. The counties are pressing for regional financing for operations and for county and municipal control of the commission. There are now 37 parks and park reserves in the regional system, with seven more being acquired and developed, and seven others envisioned. This would produce a system of 56,500 acres by the year 2000. Somewhat curiously, the council has not been centrally involved in several unique facilities which might be thought of a uniquely of metropolitan interest. It stayed away from the intensely political battle over a new domed, and ultimately downtown, stadium. It has had little to do with the new Minnesota state zoo. A proposal for an Olympic-sized speedskating track has been assigned to it for study.

Housing.

The council's involvement in housing has leaned heavily toward the supply and dispersal of subsidized units for low-income families. Its most controversial decision, in 1971, was to down-rate applications from cities for federal aid for any purpose if the municipality did not have an adequate program for low-income housing. Partly as a result, the regional proportion of subsidized units located in the central cities dropped from 90 percent in 1971 to 60 percent in 1979; and the number of suburbs with subsidized housing rose from ten to 99. The council, as a regional Housing Redevelopment Authority (HRA), will administer Section 8 programs for suburbs not wishing to establish their own agency. A staff proposal to move into the construction of large units for low-income families was rejected by the Council in 1979. There has been a great deal of work on the cost of zoning and building regulations. The Council is less involved in other housing policy issues in the region, such as the 1981 rent-control debate in Minneapolis, and in the larger strategic questions of new construction in a region oversupplied with three-bedroom homes housing one and two-person families.

Health.

The year 1981 saw a boiling controversy over efforts by the Metropolitan Council and by the Metropolitan Health Board to restrain hospital investment and actually to reduce the supply of hospitals and hospital beds. The Twin Cities area is a leader in efforts, primarily by the business community, to reduce the expensive utilization of hospitals, largely through the expansion of prepaid arrangements, admission screening, and length of stay reviews. The region has a large hospital system of about 11,000 beds. An almost identical region, Seattle-Tacoma, by contrast, operates with about 6,500 beds. The demand-reduction efforts are producing a surplus of bed capacity, which the council and the Health Board have been attempting to reduce by resisting the construction of new hospitals in the suburbs and by proposing the closing of existing hospitals in the central areas.[2] Outraged hospitals have appealed politically to the governor. Regulation and governmental action appear unable to stop large, appealing and vigorously promoted hospital capital projects. The council and the Health Board are, as a result, now leaning toward the greater use of market forces such as the elimination of public subsidies or changes in the system by which hospitals can be reimbursed for almost anything they do. At stake is a health-care system spending roughly two billion dollars a year in the Twin Cities area and growing at a compound rate of 12 percent a year. The increase alone exceeds all the property tax in the region.

Communications.

In an unusual move for regional agencies, the council got involved in cable-television planning around 1970. Partly as a result, Minnesota is the only state to have laid in a planning framework prior to the arrival of the industry later in the decade.[3] Franchising, under the 1973 state law, must occur in the metropolitan area after the creation of cable service territories which ensure that all municipalities are included in an orderly way. There are, in addition, requirements for the interconnection of all service areas into a regionwide arrangement for distributing programs. The actual construction of cable has been slow, not so much because of the planning process as because of the intense competition among companies for entry to this high-income market. Fifty and even 100-channel proposals are not uncommon along with substantial provision for local access. Work by the council's advisory committee also ensured that considerations for regional unity will also enter into decisions about measured service pricing, as that is introduced by the telephone company. Curiously, the council terminated its activity in communications in 1978, just prior to the major play in cable franchises. (In 1982 it is moving to revive it.)

Education and Social Services.

The council has not done anything regarding the school system. Education in Minnesota is organized independently of general government. The expansion of schools was adequately handled by the local districts, the trouble started when enrollments began declining in the 1970s. The schools were slow to respond to the demographic changes which could have been better anticipated.

The council tried but did not find a way to become significantly involved effectively in the area of social service delivery. Its Social Framework effort, from 1975 to 1978, was an effort to develop a metropolitan role in service delivery or needs assessment and planning, but it was resisted, especially by the counties. The monitoring role eventually proposed proved unappealing, and the council terminated the program.

Governmental Structure.

Between 1967 and 1976, the council brought to the legislature a series of proposals for the construction of the metropolitan level of government itself. But even though the gradual incorporation of the entire 7-county area is creating essentially two levels of front-line local government for the policy-making and service relationships between counties and municipalities, it has not been active on the structure and functions of counties and municipalities.

The state had taken over the annexation and incorporation process through the Minnesota Municipal Commission (MMC) in 1959. The council provides help to the MMC in its work. The turf issues in questions of government structure are too great for a metropolitan agency that needs local government cooperation.

Airports.

The Twin Cities area system is the sixth largest in the world with one major air-carrier field, a secondary field for private jets and five fields for light planes to relieve the major airports. Created in 1943 when competition between the two cities literally produced scheduled airline service from Minneapolis to St. Paul, the Metropolitan Airports Commission (MAC) was a powerful agency when the Metropolitan Council appeared. It is the subject of the most minimal council involvement in its finances and membership. In a major 1969 decision, however, the council twice vetoed the MAC's proposal for a new, second major air-carrier field in the northern suburbs. The MAC is now heavily dependent on the Council for the coordination of land-use decisions that will ensure the preservation of flight corridors around its existing major airport. The MAC has been slow to acquire other sites for satellite airports and has not been helped significantly by the council, which has basically waited for MAC to take the lead.

Finance.

Changes in the systems of taxation and state aid have been an absolutely central part of the legislature's policy for the unification of the metropolitan area. The sales tax was introduced, statewide, in 1967, with a part of the revenues returned to cities and to schools on a population basis. This set a pattern of statewide uniform rates, with revenues returned by a formula on an increasingly complex and equalizing basis. Local sales and income taxes were prohibited in 1971, locking in this policy. That year, too, the legislature set up a program for the limited sharing of the growth of the commercial and industrial tax base. Since 1971, 40 percent of the net increase in nonresidential valuations has been held out from entering directly into the tax base of the jurisdictions in which the property is located. Instead, the funds were pooled at the regional level and reallocated on a formula reflecting population and related inversely to valuation per capita. More than a billion dollars of market value is now in the pool, and the range of disparities in dollars of valuation per capita among municipalities has been reduced from roughly eleven to one to less than six to one.[4]

The Metropolitan Council typically does not make legislative proposals respecting the system for state aid and local finance. On a number of occasions in recent years, the council has held back even from taking a position on requests for financing brought to the legislature by the Metropolitan Transit Commission. The council reviews the user charges which are the principal means of financing the sewerage system and represent about 40 percent of transit finance. Through its investment framework, largely a monitoring function, it keeps track of public expenditure in the region.

The Metropolitan Council performs a large number of other tasks. It distributes money to arts programs, and it has negotiated an agreement on a regional system for emergency services and the 911 telephone dialing system. It makes plans, does studies, keeps statistics, and publishes and distributes maps and reports.

THE GENERAL DEVELOPMENT PLAN

Prior to the Metropolitan Council's existence, there was only a regional planning commission and a good deal of talk about shaping the region as a whole. The development guide laid before the new council when formed in 1967 was, however, not accepted by this more political body. There was, in any event, no capacity to implement it as the sewage, transportation, housing, and other programs and agencies remained to be constructed.

By the early 1970s, however, with these programs and agencies in place, the question of the overall plan resurfaced before the council, which was acting as the regional architect and general contractor. In 1974-75, the older, wiser, and more politically realistic council worked out a new development framework which was enacted by the legislature in the Land Planning Act of 1976 and is now in the late stages of implementation. It is considered to be the most comprehensive attempt at growth management in any metropolitan area in the nation.

Its strategy was largely shaped by one council member, a former city council member in the largest suburb in the region, and a developer's attorney. It began with a realization that the Metropolitan Council could influence the development of the region, but not control it, certainly not centrally. It could not coerce municipalities in the same manner as municipalities can coerce private developers whose money-clocks are running. It must work with and through municipalities. The idea was two-fold. First, the council was to establish a Metropolitan Urban Service Area (MUSA), a portion of the metropolitan area beyond which development would not be permitted, at least not at metropolitan expense. Also, the council was to come to a decision about what capacity would and would not be provided in the systems for which it is responsible, at what location, and on what date. Second, municipalities were to be required to prepare and adopt local comprehensive plans, including capital development programs, that would neither over use nor under use those metropolitan facilities. Municipalities would thus detail the MUSA line as it passed through their territory throughout the developed portion of the seven-county region and the municipal system of zoning and building control thus put to the implementation of the regional plan. Essentially, it is a strategy of in-filling which limits expansion contiguously around the fringe of the Twin Cities urban area.

The opposition of fringe area suburbs and of the housing industry, which was concerned about higher land and housing prices, was overcome in the passage of the 1976 act. The metropolitan systems statements were adopted on schedule with the major decision involving the elimination of any further thought of a second major airport. Local planning was slow but, drawn along by $2 million in state planning funds from the council to local units, is now close to completion. A strong agricultural preservation program was installed for the ring of land outside the MUSA but within the seven-county region. The council is just now beginning to face up to the tough implications of this program. There is a need to keep the production of housing units in line with new-household formation during the 1980s. Its decision to cut off movement to land beyond the urban fringe will oblige the council to join the housing industry in pressing politically for higher-density development on the remaining open land within the MUSA.

In all this development planning, the Metropolitan Council has been predominantly suburban oriented. It has given some attention to the fully developed area. However, the ring of redevelopment activity around the old central cores of Minneapolis and St. Paul is still physically within the central city boundaries and is being handled by these municipal governments. Even the council's early thoughts of assisting in the development of the major centers emerging around both cities' central business districts has been quietly laid aside.

SUMMARY AND EVALUATION

The change wrought by the legislature with these metropolitan institutions seems a permanent one. Certainly they have proved to be a major part of the Twin Cities area's success. Criticism arises anew with each succeeding generation of local officials and legislators, many of whom do not remember the troubles before the council which led to its creation. Each time challenges arise, as they have again in 1981, the issue returns to the legislature for a study which reaffirms the necessity of these policies. This relationship with the state is fundamental and is essentially a relationship with the legislature. The governors have shown only passing interest.

The most important thing that the Metropolitan Council does is to make political decisions, as it did again in 1981 in working out a compromise on design to permit construction of a major freeway from the west into the Minneapolis downtown, and from the south into central St. Paul. The council does not seek out such issues as aggressively as it once did, but it will do its duty when asked. Clearly, it was right to build the council for this policy-making purpose, rather than to create, as in Toronto, a development machine without adequate ability to resolve political conflict.[5]

Like most governments, the council is mainly reactive to events and to proposals from others. A proper view would therefore include as a part of any system of regional planning and governance those outside, nongovernmental institutions that are politically independent enough and sufficiently well informed to function as the raisers of issues which political people will have to resolve. The Metropolitan Council can be counted as a political body even though its membership is not now nor in the foreseeable future likely to be determined by election.[6]

The Metropolitan Council's relationship with the federal government has been a difficult one. It will continue to be difficult since Washington works with a municipal definition of the city rather than a metropolitan definition. This has not been a major problem for the Metropolitan Council, which has managed to resist the federal government's preference for a Council of Governments arrangement, and which has its own charter and financing from state legislation. It is, in truth, more of a problem for the federal government, especially now as it cuts back the financing of local government, than for the Minneapolis-St. Paul region.

After 1960, American cities had a choice. Recognizing that the urban regions are, after all, the great centers of wealth in this country, they could have gone for reorganization, for new governmental and fiscal arrangements designed to release those available resources of money and of leadership locally, in order to solve urban problems. Or, they could have left in place the existing boundaries and local fiscal arrangements, and sought the financing for the distressed areas and for the redeveloping central cities from the outside. After some unsuccessful efforts at metropolitan reorganization in Cleveland and St. Louis in the 1950s, most regions (Minneapolis-St. Paul excepted) chose the latter route. For these, then, it was a rational decision. It avoided the local battles over metropolitan government, and from 1960 to 1975, the federal government did provide the money.

Now with the flow of federal funds diminishing, it becomes necessary for these other areas to look again toward the resources available within the region. For most central cities, the problem is that over these past 20 years, little has been done to build constructive relationships either with their suburbs or with their state governments. The effort must start at the beginning and will be extraordinarily difficult. Not the least of the problems is that federal policy is so fundamentally confused in its failure to focus clearly on the potential that lies in the process of state law making.[7]

The Metropolitan Council was established when the Legislature in Minnesota, as in other states, was trying to deal with the problem of metropolitan growth. Today, 15 years later, the council remains primarily concerned with urban physical development. Its overwhelming challenge is to move now to help the Twin Cities area and its local governments deal with the adjustment to a new condition of nongrowth or decline in resources available to the local public sector. It is fair to say that the Metropolitan Council has not moved to this kind of leadership role. It is unfair to say that the council is at fault for this lack. It reflects the uncertainty felt throughout the community and, indeed, throughout the country about the role of government and the difficult question of public expenditure. This remains, for civic leadership, the dominant issue of the 1980s (Citizens League, 1980).

10. A Crisis in Regional Planning: The Tri-State Regional Planning Commission

Ingrid W. Reed

BACKGROUND

Tri-State in this case refers to the region surrounding New York City which includes parts of three states, New York, Connecticut, and New Jersey. It may be the most well-known region in the country or in the world. The towers of New York City surrounded by the industrial areas to the west in New Jersey, the highway and suburbs stretching out the length of Long Island to the east, and the dark hue of the green hills of Connecticut in the northern distance are a familiar picture.

How can one capture an understanding of this sprawling, complex and diverse region, let alone plan for it? With a population of 18 million and over 8 million jobs, the Tri-State region covers an area of 8,000 square miles in parts of three states. Each state has a strong governor and an independent legislature located in state capitals outside of the region.

Within this area, 600 localities and 27 counties or, in the case of Connecticut, regions, have a powerful stake in their own planning

117

agenda, as do the various state departments, federal agencies, and the many intra- and interstate bodies. For many years, New York City was considered the hub of this region. Economic and transportation ties were usually perceived as giving the tri-state area a reason to think regionally. But, what little planning was done with a regional emphasis arose outside the usual government agencies. The Regional Plan Association (RPA), the non-profit citizens' group supported by businesses and individuals, has for the past 50 years played an important role focusing on the common problems faced by the people in governmental entities surrounding New York City. It has produced two detailed regional plans and continues to conduct policy studies designed to focus attention on regional issues.

The Port Authority of New York and New Jersey is a powerful regional actor as it plans and manages transportation and port facilities in New Jersey and New York, the governors of which appoint its board. The Port Authority recently has also addressed broader regional issues such as economic development and infrastructure rehabilitation and replacement.

It was not until 1961 that the governors of Connecticut, New York, and New Jersey took a regional approach by creating the Tri-State Transportation Committee in order to address critical mass transportation problems. Four years later, this committee was upgraded to the status of an interstate commission through a compact ratified by the legislatures of the three states.

The commission was charged with responsibility for conducting surveys and studies and for submitting recommendations which address the immediate and long-range development problems of housing, transportation and other public facilities, as well as land use and other areas not specified. However, the Bylaws of the Tri-State Regional Planning Commission explicitly leave the operation of facilities and delivery of services to the states.

In the late 1960s, the Transportation Commission was given responsibility for review functions which grew out of new federal programs such as the Model Cities Act. Ten years after the first regional effort, the compact was revised by the states and its mandate broadened to make it a full-fledged regional planning commission, now known as the Tri-State Regional Planning Commission. It was designated the official Metropolitan Planning Organization (MPO) and the area-wide clearinghouse for roughly the northern half of New Jersey, New York City, New York State along the Hudson River, Long Island, and the Connecticut suburbs.

Twenty years after the initial regional approach, the governors of the states authorized an examination of the mission and structure of the commission to enable it to better meet the planning needs of the future.[1] Before looking at that critical assessment, a review of the commission is in order.

Since its inception, the commission has been controlled by the states who created it, although there is little evidence of the states directing the commission to address issues they have in common (Governor's Task Force on the Future of the Tri-State Regional Planning Commission, 1981). The states appear to be preoccupied with making certain that Tri-State meets the growing regulations and requirements of federal programs to keep funds coming to the states and localities. The commission lacks the autonomy to address regional issues since it depends on the states for resources and policy direction (Danielson and Doig, 1982). In 1978, the governor of New York successfully maneuvered to get the two Long Island counties out of Tri-State's direct A-95 review process, an indication of the powerful role of a governor in the Tri-State structure.

Although more than 75 percent of the Tri-State's annual budget represents federal programs, the required matching funds come from states, localities, and agencies. The general expenditures for continuing programs, supported by federal programs such as the Department of Housing and Urban Development (HUD) Section 701 and the Urban Mass Transportation Administration, are matched with state funds based on a formula in the compact. This requires that New York State supply 45 percent, New Jersey 45 percent, and Connecticut ten percent of the funds. The formula was negotiated to reflect Connecticut's low percentage of the population in the region. New Jersey and New York share responsibility for the major portion although New York by far has the largest population.[2] If one state should consider withholding funds, as a New Jersey agency has already recommended to the governor, it would jeopardize the amount HUD could award to Tri-State since the 45-45-10 ratio must be retained.

New York state has the unique role of banker in the Tri-State financial structure. Based on an annual budget, New York state makes funds available, under the first-instance appropriation provision, until the state and federal agencies are billed by Tri-State on the basis of authorized grants. According to records of the

State of New York, the amount repaid in recent years has fallen far short of that expended. Consequently, New York is indicating its reluctance to play the role of up-front banker, and in 1980–81, it reduced Tri-State's budget and demanded specific cuts in personnel items.

The State of Connecticut did not limit itself to budget threats. Unhappy with Tri-State's perceived interference in local matters since the 1970s, various initiatives in the legislature called for Connecticut to break away from the compact. The most recent initiatives during the summer of 1981 resulted in taking transportation planning for Connecticut out of Tri-State's jurisdiction and turning it over to the state's planning regions. The legislature reluctantly authorized a $100,000 contribution for strategic planning and agreed to participate in the commission until May 1982.

The commission which governs Tri-State is made up of 15 commissioners, five appointed by the governor of each state under the rules that vary by state. Each governor names two state officials who serve ex-officio and three public members representative of subregions. The compact requires that one of the New York state commissioners be the chairperson of the New York City Planning Commission.

Decisions of the commission are by majority vote, but the minutes are open for ten days to provide for review by the governors. Any one governor can exercise veto power over the minutes and thereby the actions of the commission. Further, the commission's executive committee, which approves A-95 reviews and staff reports before they are passed on to the full commission, is composed of the state officials who head programs directly affected by the decisions made by the Tri-State Commission.

ACTIVITIES

Given the constraints of addressing regional issues, it is not surprising that the Tri-State Commission's accomplishments in its ten-year history are considered routine and undistinguished. It has produced the required regional plans for transportation, housing, and land use and has conducted the A-95 review activities. However, according to the RPA, "the staff performs like a consulting firm, primarily providing data and responding to study requests of state and federal agencies. They seldom take the initiative to raise hard issues for commission consideration, and little of their research reaches the public" (Danielson and Doig, 1982).

The Tri-State planning staff and commission have found that carrying out the ongoing comprehensive planning process, even in a perfunctory way, raises the fears of the localities that Tri-State is dictating policies to the local governments. At the same time, Tri-State has been pressured by citizen groups to use its plans to promote social and environmental goals. Often these goals are resisted by local governments. This was particularly the case with housing policy.

Tri-State became caught in a crosscurrent. On the one hand, it was forced to implement detailed requirements of federal government programs which resulted in tons of reports and papers, ever more detailed numbers and projections. On the other hand, the staff was pressed for definitive studies on such controversial state issues, admittedly of regional significance, as the Hackensack Meadowlands and the Westway Project. It apeared that most of Tri-State's work was irrelevant in the sense that it collected data and prepared technical reports that did not serve the needs of the localities. When it did attempt to be relevant, it intruded on issues that only one of the states could decide.

The Governors' Task Force on the Future of the Tri-State Regional Planning Commission was the result of the commission itself recognizing that it had to sort out the criticism coming from two fronts: those who thought Tri-State did too little too ineffectively and those who thought an overly activist role not sufficiently helpful to existing governments was being played by Tri-State.

REDIRECTION

Is there a unique role which the Tri-State Regional Planning Commission can play and which other entities cannot? Is there a rationale for a regional planning agency to fulfill the needs that states and localities cannot meet themselves?

The Governors' Task Force, in its report in January 1981, affirmed the need but stressed that it was essential to redirect the mission of the Tri-State to provide "strategic regional planning" and to reorganize the commission so that it can perform that major function.

The Task Force was composed of five citizens appointed by each of the governors. Over a 15 month period of study, it looked at the past and present operation of Tri-State, conducted a questionnaire survey of 1,650 elected officials, planning professionals, and citizen activists (Duke, 1981), and held numerous public forums and interviews with federal, state, and local officials.

The Task Force found no support for turning Tri-State into a regional government or for assigning it a role in which it merely provided routine service to governments. Given the documented deficiencies and the lack of strong support for the Tri-State Commission, the Task Force considered recommending the dissolution of that agency in favor of creating a new entity. However, because of the difficulties in maintaining eligibility for federal funding and the possible increase in cost of clearinghouse functions if transferred to the states, a change in emphasis was sought instead. The Task Force recommended that the central mission of Tri-State should be the analysis and public communication of issues "that can affect future events and resources of the whole region . . . . Its objective is to help people and governments make rational transitions from present to future." The Task Force recognized that state and local governments needed a regional resource to examine regional issues such as movement of jobs, energy needs, water supplies, capital to meet demands for new construction and maintenance, and impact of the international economy.

The Task Force stressed the organizational changes that had to accompany the redirection of its mission. The changes include :

1. In order to eliminate conflicts of interest and improve performance, commissioners should not be appointed on an ex-officio basis but on the basis of time available and interest in the regional agency;
2. In recognition of the limited powers of the commission each state should assume more responsibility for implementing federally mandated activities;
3. The budget and financial activities should be systematized and open for public review;
4. Inactive standing committees should be abolished; and
5. A new structure of public participation should be put in place.

Recognizing that these changes might not be easy to implement, the Task Force urged "the federal government to recognize that the region is not a typical metropolitan area" and to assist in planning alternatives for project review activities.

The Task Force findings and recommendations went before the Commission's special committee on redirection which was given six months to reach consensus on how to proceed with the recommendations of the Task Force. In the meantime, the Tri-State staff was significantly reduced by budget cuts at the federal and state levels. When the Task Force began its work in 1979, Tri-State had 227 staff members. This number was cut to 170 in January 1981, and to 100 in the fall and 70 at the end of 1981. The continuing planning program budget which was $3.8 million in 1978–79 now stands at $3.1 million. It is supported by Section 701 Comprehensive Planning funds which are scheduled to end in 1982-83.

The remaining staff did not appear to have been influenced by the Task Force recommendations even though the recommendations have been received favorably by the commission, the RPA and others well known for monitoring Tri-State. Two areas where significant improvements could have been made in response to the Task Force, the description of its work program and the provision of a unified external audit, remain unaddressed.[3]

The recommendations for change may be difficult to carry out, but outside influences continue to shape a redirection of the agency. The Reagan program has shifted the responsibility for meeting most federal requirements to the states and localities. Block grants to the states are fostering new planning arrangements, although transportation budgets still include regional planning requirements.

Furthermore, there may be a growing realization that the Snow Belt states are at a disadvantage in competing with the Sun Belt states, causing the entities in the Tri-State region to identify critical concerns and band together to press for the public sector and private sector resources required to avoid stagnation and encourage development.

New insight among the leaders in the region may cause them to see that its health and vitality depend on a stronger linkage of the parts of the region with the rest of the world. The towers of New York City, while still dominating the image of the region, no longer are the main focus of the region. The substantial centers of commerce spread throughout the region (New York City is only one of several) may need to find a way to confront on a regional basis the strategic planning issues that the states cannot deal with individually.

THE FUTURE

The Tri-State Commission's Committee for Redirection made its report to the commission in November 1981, as scheduled. Although labeled "semifinal," the report, on the one hand, endorsed the purposes of regional planning and the approach outlined by the Task Force. On the other hand, it rejected the recommendations for changing the structure of the commission and the type of leadership required to fulfill the purposes.

The lack of attention to leadership issues was particularly distressing to the Task Force in light of the fact that the commission continued to lack a quorum for its meetings and had not taken constructive actions to devise operating procedures for the executive committee, nor to develop a mechanism for public participation.

The commission also had not made significant progress in establishing financial accountability for the organization. The promised changes in the accounting system did not materialize, and the commission's finance subcommittee had not addressed the serious problems of a lack of a budget, audited statement of accounts or a financial report. However, the commission had contracted with Peat, Marwick, and Mitchell which relied on the Task Force's pieced-together financial reports for its analysis, for a preliminary report on its financial system. The firm's report cited a number of deficiencies (Peat, Marwick, and Mitchell, 1981).

On December 14, 1981, after reviewing its studies and the reform efforts of the commission, the Task Force concluded that there was no alternative except to return to its original assessment that the existing agency served the region adequately. The Task Force, in a letter to the governors of the three states, affirmed its support for a "continuing strategic regional planning effort," but recommended that Tri-State should be abolished and a new effort be undertaken to develop a regional agency more appropriate to current needs. The Task Force called on the three governors to meet and "create a working group of their representatives and business, labor and community leaders to develop a new regional framework for cooperation."[4]

Given the financial problems of Tri-State, it also recommended that the governors appoint a Financial Oversight Committee to supervise the final settlement of accounts. Since Connecticut had already assumed contract obligations for transportation planning, similar arrangements were urged upon the other two states.

No official reaction has come from the governors or the commission. Governor Byrne was quoted in the *Newark Star Ledger* on December 15, 1981, as not surprised by the recommendation because he expressed fears about the agency's competence when the Task Force was established. The executive director of Tri-State affirmed his confidence in the agency and cited the constructive accommodations to budget cuts and staff reductions.

As of December 1981, Connecticut still plans to withdraw from the compact in May 1982. New Jersey has a new governor reportedly overwhelmed with a multitude of reports focusing on problems facing the incoming administration. New York's commission members have been the strongest supporters of the status quo, but that may not remain firm if reports confirm his state's deficit from the lack of reimbursements for first-instance appropriations made by New York.

It is not hard to predict that in time the weak, ineffective agency may be dissolved, and organized regional planning in the tri-state area may come to an end. What will take its place is uncertain since there is still no strong drive within the states to recognize their self-interests in effective regional planning that strategically addresses the problems all three must confront in the 1980s.

IMPLICATIONS FOR REGIONAL PLANNING

The tri-state region can easily be written off as atypical and not relevant to the discussion of the future of regional planning. It is larger than any other designated planning regions. An interstate arrangement of three states is a particularly complicated one. New York City as a national and international center cannot easily be balanced with the interests of other entities in the region.

On the other hand, the spread-out nature of development in the post-World War II era has created other regions that include hundreds of square miles. Many American cities grew up on the banks of rivers with regional development occurring in more than one state. Often large cities play a dominant role in regions.

If regional approaches to planning are to make significant contributions to shaping development and providing services, designs must be found that include constructive multistate direction of regional agencies, and new management principles, including public participation, that can guide these regional agencies.

The tri-state experience may prove to be an example of what not to do, in two specific respects: in the structure and functioning of the governing body, and in the financial organization and administrative direction of the regional agency. In Tri-State's case, if either of these had been stronger and more creative, the Tri-State region could today have been the example of what can be accomplished through a regional planning approach, even under circumstances that are unwieldly and complex.

11. The Metropolitan Service District (METRO)

Denton U. Kent

Denton U. Kent

HISTORY OF PORTLAND'S AREAWIDE APPROACH TO GOVERNANCE

A form of government, new not only to the Portland metropolitan area in Oregon but to the nation as well, began operation on January 1, 1979. Its creation followed passage by the voters of a measure which called for the reorganization of the Metropolitan Service District (MSD) to absorb the planning functions of the Columbia Region Association of Governments (CRAG) and in the process establish a directly elected regional governing body. The new regional government is popularly referred to as METRO.

METRO is the result of an evolutionary process that extends back to the early 1960s in the Portland metropolitan area. CRAG was created as a result of a governmental reorganization study in 1963 sponsored by the Oregon state legislature, and formed to study the inadequacies of the Metropolitan Planning Commission. The original CRAG was a voluntary association of governments comprised of four counties and 14 cities. It sought to identify regional problems and needs, and to prepare and adopt regional plans. The early CRAG placed strong emphasis on intergovernmental cooperation. The association pursued a policy of giving full recognition to the plans of its member jurisdictions. This approach, of course, had a major disadvantage; it glossed over conflicts between local jurisdictions. CRAG's low key approach came under criticism as it became evident that farm land and natural resources were being lost at an alarming rate, new commercial centers were having a negative impact on existing ones, and the public costs of serving uncontrolled growth skyrocketed.

By the early 1970s, a new approach to regional development was being called for in the community. This local sentiment, coupled with a strong drive for environmental protection and land-use controls at the state level, resulted in the 1973 Oregon legislature passing two bills directly affecting regionalism in the Portland metropolitan area.

The first bill, referred to as Senate Bill 100, established a state land-use and development process which, in addition to specifying that all local jurisdictions would create comprehensive plans directly addressing state land-use and development, set up local coordination mechanisms to assure local plan's compliance to those state standards. CRAG became the coordinating body for the local plans produced in the Portland metropolitan area. The second bill passed by the state legislature focused on Portland and made membership of local jurisdictions in the CRAG association mandatory. Previously, under the voluntary system, a jurisdiction could withdraw both its participation and financing if they felt disadvantaged by a particular position taken by the regional body. Under the new system, there was a recognition of the existence of a unique regional interest and also the fact that local interests were inextricably intertwined. The legislation further provided that CRAG could overrule or send back a local development plan which did not conform with regional comprehensive or functional plans. The organizational structure of the reconstituted CRAG changed little from the original one, with the board of directors and general assembly being comprised of members of local jurisdictions' elected policy boards.

While the CRAG was developing as the primary focus of regional development planning, other areawide agencies, generally of a single purpose nature, were actively being formed to manage the affairs of the metropolitan area. For example, in 1969, the MSD was formed as an operational entity to deal with solid waste disposal issues, to implement the work in drainage initiated by CRAG, and to assume the operation of the zoo through a regionwide rather than a local tax base. Its creation was the result of a popular vote and its board comprised of representatives of local governments. The Port of Portland has evolved from a Docks Commission and operates marine ports, airports, and some economic development activities under a policy board appointed by the governor. The Tri-County Metropolitan Transit District (Tri-Met) was formulated under a gubernatorial appointment process after the state legislature passed enabling legislation for transit districts in 1969. Also created by the 1969 legislature was the Portland Metropolitan Area Local Government Boundary Commission. The commission, again made up of gubernatorial appointments, was charged with guiding the growth of cities, special districts, and Oregon's metropolitan communities through dealing with service extensions, annexations, and the creation, dissolution, or unification of cities and special districts. Under federal legislative initiatives, a multicounty health planing agency was also formed. Therefore, as of 1973, six major agencies existed, each dealing with a specific function or set of services in the areawide governance.

This proliferation resulted in functional fragmentation as well as creating a system of regional or areawide agencies which were free from broad political control, remote from the citizens, and did not provide for any direct voter participation in their governance process. Mounting public frustration and concern with the solution to areawide problems and an unsuccessful attempt at a city-county merger created the atmosphere in which a fundamental change in the areawide structure could be explored.

In 1975, the opportunity to make such an exploration manifested itself through the National Academy of Public Administration (NAPA). NAPA, in conjunction with the U.S. Department of Housing and Urban Development (HUD), announced the availability of two $100,000 grants to study urban needs and services and assess which ones are better implemented on a regional level and which are best performed by local jurisdictions, and to make recommendations for implementation of such a two-tier government.

An *ad hoc* Portland group, many members of which had previously been involved in governmental reform movements, decided to submit an application, and after a rigorous selection process the Portland area was awarded one of the grants. Subsequently, a 65-member commission, representing all phases of the community, known as the Tri-County Citizens Committee, was formed and

$50,000 in local matching funds were raised. The commission then began to work on its proposal for "politically accountable regionalism." After approximately one year's work, the commission reported its recommendations and prepared to lobby for their enactment through the 1977 legislature. While the proposal was modified in some particulars and not directly implemented by the legislature as was originally intended, the legislature did agree to submit the concept for referendum.

THE STRUCTURE AND FUNCTION OF METRO

The most striking feature of the proposal submitted to the voters was the creation of a popularly elected, 12-member council and an elected executive officer. The council, representing districts of approximately 74,000 people, holds the legislative and policy perogatives of the agency. The executive officer, elected at large, holds the policy-implementation function and has no vote on the council. In this way, the proposal built in the direct political accountability the Tri-County commission was seeking. To implement the proposal, a popular vote was to be taken on the issue to merge CRAG and MSD and structure the new agency on the MSD foundation. One unfortunate offshoot of this model was that Clark County, Washington, an integral part of the Portland Metropolitan area and a member of CRAG, was not provided for in the reorganization plan. Another significant geographic feature of the proposed new agency was the reduction of the proposed boundaries from the entire three-county service area to the urban and urbanizing portions of these counties.

The general functions to be provided by the new entity included both those previously held by the MSD and CRAG, as well as the provision for some new service options. MSD now held the power to acquire, construct, alter, maintain and operate interceptor trunk and outfall sewers and piping stations, and facilities for treatment and disposal of sewage. It had the power to dispose of and provide facilities for disposal of solid and liquid wastes. MSD acted to control the flow and provide for the drainage of surface waters by means of dams, ditches, dikes, canals, and similar necessary improvements. Additionally, it was to provide public transportation and terminal facilities for public transportation, and to operate and maintain zoo facilities.

Similar to the responsibilities once held by CRAG, METRO's statute sets out the following mandates:

1. Adopt regional land-use planning goals and objectives;
2. Serve as the plan review and coordination body for land use and planning activities within the district; and
3. Adopt functional plans for air quality, water quality, transportation, and other areas and activities having significant impact upon the development of the metropolitan area.

In addition, with voter approval of a tax base or income tax, METRO would be allowed, though not required, to assume new areas of responsibility. These could include acquiring, developing, altering, and operating water supply and distribution systems. It could take the responsibility to plan, coordinate, and evalute the provision of human services including programs for aging, health care, manpower, mental health, and children and youth. Further, it now could take the responsibility for the provision of open spaces and recreation facilities, and multipurpose complexes for sports, conventions, and entertainment. Also, it can furnish adult and juvenile justice programs and facilities and provide various local support facilities. The new regional government could also assume local aspects of functions with agreement of affected local governments. New functions can be assumed with voter approval.

The merger of the various single purpose, areawide agencies were each treated differently in the question to be put before the voters. First, CRAG and MSD were to be directly merged; the new entity could order the transfer of the transit system and its control (Tri-Met) to itself at any time. The Boundary Commission could only be absorbed by an affirmative popular vote. Combining the port in the new structure had successfully been opposed at the legislature by port interests and therefore remained a free-standing agency. The Health Services Agency was deemed, by the Tri-County Local Government Commission, as more private than public and so was not recommended for merger.

The question went to the voters in May of 1978, and passed by a combined three-county majority of 55 percent.[1] The question failed in one county. The county subsequently filed suit to remove themselves from METRO but was unsuccessful.

FINANCING METRO

The enabling legislation sets up broad taxation, assessment, and bonding powers. With voter approval, METRO may establish a property tax base, and income tax, or a corporate business tax. METRO may impose fees and charges for user services and issue revenue and general obligation bonds. In practice, METRO has used the tax base power only for financing of the zoo. METRO also collects user charges for solid waste operations and for the zoo, with the remainder of its activities funded primarily from assessments on local governments, which serve as matching funds for the leverage of a variety of federal and state grants-in-aid, and also provide for a small portion of general operating expenses. The ability to levy an assessment on local jurisdictions expired on July 1, 1981, under the original enabling legislation. While the amount of money involved, some $550,000, is small compared to the total budget, it is the only source of flexible funding with which the agency can direct the priority of its planning and development programs. An attempt was made in 1980 to pass a tax base for METRO to replace these local funds. That measure was defeated by an almost two-to-one margin, even though with the state property tax relief program in Oregon the tax base could have been established at no net increase in cost to local taxpayers. Consequently, efforts were successfully made in the 1981 legislative session to extend METRO's ability to levy assessments on local jurisdictions for an additional four-year period.

FUNCTIONAL ISSUES AND ROLES

METRO has now been in existence for over two and one-half years. In some areas, METRO has maintained the functional emphasis held by it predecessor agencies, and in others, there has been a marked change. The following portrays the current status of a variety of issues that METRO is addressing.

Transportation.
METRO is federally designated as the lead transportation planning agency for the region. It is required by its enabling legislation to prepare a functional plan for transportation and under the same legislation can assume the operation of Tri-Met's public transportation system. METRO has three basic roles which are discharged in

the transportation function. First, it provides technical support by evaluating the use and effectiveness of the region. Additionally, METRO serves as coordinator for the regional transportation plan by providing a framework for local jurisdiction's plans and policies. Finally, METRO authorizes all federal transportation funds available to the region for transit and highways. This responsibility is made more significant since the Portland area has withdrawn over $500 million in Interstate Highway Funding and rescheduled that funding to foster locally determined, higher priority transportation projects.

A number of mobility, economic, land-use, environmental, social and energy issues are directly affected by the region's transportation system. In many cases, these can only be addressed at the regional level due to the fact that transportation problems do not respect jurisdictional boundaries. Transit, highways, and streets are major public investments which need to be incorporated into a comprehensive regional capital improvement plan.

Land Use.

METRO is designated by statute as the area planning coordination agency. This means that METRO reviews and coordinates the comprehensive plans of 27 local jurisdictions, resolves conflicts, and ensures consistency between the local plans and state and regional goals. Further, METRO has formulated and adopted a regional Urban Growth Containment Boundary which delineates the extent of urban-level development and provides for the preservation of scarce farm and forest resources. In addition, a Land Use Framework Element is in place which establishes appropriate uses, facilities and services for areas outside of the urban growth boundary. A specialized project to maximize transit investment through supportive land-use patterns is underway. Related aspects of transportation, air quality, and land-use planning work are integrated.

The waning interest and popularity of the state land-use planning program is being reflected in a less aggressive planning role being taken by METRO. The continuance of programs to streamline the development process within the growth boundary needs to be pursued as does the review of major amendments to local comprehensive plans. These functions can only be carried out effectively at the regional level. Similarly, a continuing monitoring process to measure availability of land for urban development needs to be pursued. A coordinated system for assessing public investment impacts on land development patterns needs to be established.

Economic Development.

From the outset, METRO defined its involvement in economic development from a general welfare perspective. The concept of equating economic development with employment growth, increased average incomes, or reduced unemployment was rejected in favor of an approach relating to the efficiency of urban forms and the quality of the urban environment. Under this philosophy, the major projects undertaken include Urban Growth Boundary maintenance, analysis of the price effect of the boundary on the market place, the availability of public facilities on decisions for industrial and commercial centers, and establishing the type of future housing requirements to meet forecasted employment and income levels. Some attempts at coordination of economic development plans by local jurisdictions have been made but have not been successful due to political chauvinism.

There is a need to end the current lack in coordination of economic development efforts among the local jurisdictions. A system for realistically addressing the availability and supply of commercial and industrial land is a logical first step in that process. Continued fragmentation in economic development activities will stifle the maximization of public investments in the infrastructure and support services. The private sector linkage with the public sector must be strengthened.

Housing.

METRO has the lead role in determining fair-share allocation of publicly supported housing. It has adopted an areawide Housing Opportunity Plan and is working on a plan for housing goals and policies. A regional standard for the split of single vs. multifamily housing new construction and average density levels has been established by METRO and is being monitored for compliance.

Currently, there is no method for allocation of market-level housing. The cost of new housing and the cessation of some federal housing programs exacerbate the housing dilemma for the low income population. Condominium conversions have had a negative impact on the availability of rental units needed for a variety of rental housing demands.

Sewers.

METRO is the federally designated areawide 208 water quality planning agency. A 208 waste treatment management plan has been adopted and updated. Local coordination, plan review and A-95 review add to the ability to coordinate sewer and treatment plant construction.

There is an unfulfilled need to provide the infrastructure necessary to support desired land use and growth policy implementation. Existing treatment facilities are reaching capacity at a time when federal support for new facilities is drying up. Sewers need to be included in a coordinated capital improvements plan and a local source of funding must be developed.

Energy Planning.

Building on a history of several years' efforts in developing information on various aspects of regional energy analysis and the commissioning of a study of METRO's potential energy role in the early 1980s, no consensus has been reached as to what METRO, as a regional agency, should do in the energy arena. Recent efforts at coordinating requests for funding from the Bonneville Power Administration to local governments have been successful only as long as the local jurisdictions' requests are not revised or prioritized one against another.

Local jurisdictions, other than the City of Portland, are apathetic toward energy matters. This has resulted in a weakening of the energy conservation plan for the City of Portland. There is a growing public, and therefore political, perception that there is no energy crisis; consequently, elected politicians are reluctant to take a strong role in the field.

Drainage.

METRO's legislative authority allows it to deal with drainage and flood control matters. To this end, METRO declared the Johnson Creek Basin, which is contained within five separate jurisdictions, an area of regional concern in an effort to solve a 25-year-old flooding problem. METRO chose to establish a Local Improvement District (LID) and assess property owners within the LID for flood improvements. Citizens' reactions against this approach were formidable, and METRO has not instituted the financial mechanisms to deal with this problem. An urban run-off component is included in the 208 Water Quality Plan. Substantial citizen education programs are being considered.

Increased urban development is negatively impacting the quantity and quality of water in urban streams, decreasing their resource value and increasing the frequency and damage costs of flood events. Local government boundaries do not often cover the entire drainage basin, and no state or federal management program exists. Therefore, the region must deal with these problems as part of a regional development capital improvements consideration.

Criminal Justice Planning.

METRO is authorized to perform planning, coordination and financing of approved criminal justice programs. With voter approval of a tax base, METRO could build and operate detention facilities and provide direct criminal justice services. Activities include developing an overall framework plan for criminal justice system improvement, collecting and analyzing data relating to the establishment of a regional jail and developing special programs to deal with juvenile justice and jail overcrowding.

There are not statutory requirements for emergency services and justice agencies to coordinate their services. The large public budgets expended on these services require coordination to avoid duplication and waste. Construction and operation of detention facilities are inadequate in terms of facility size and humane treatment.

Zoo.

The Washington Park Zoo is a humane, scientifically based, and conservation-oriented zoological park, which provides recreation and education for the citizens within the metropolitan region. The zoo is open every day of the year and provides outreach services to schools, parks, nursing homes, and community groups throughout the METRO area.

The zoo was brought into the regional service portfolio through recognition that a facility which provides recreation and educational opportunities for the whole region should be funded by the whole region. Efforts to secure adequate capital for the zoo development have been successful, but it may be more difficult in the future as the zoo is viewed by many as a nonessential government service.

Solid Waste.

State statutes authorize METRO to plan, construct and operate solid waste disposal facilities. METRO can also control the flow of solid waste, franchise disposal facilities, impose fees, and sell industrial development revenue bonds to fund construction of solid waste disposal facilities. The original MSD agency developed and approved a solid waste management plan in 1974. This program stresses waste reduction, resource recovery, and less reliance on landfills through recycling. MSD initiated efforts toward building a resource recovery plant in 1977. Upon its formation, METRO assumed responsibility for disposal of approximately 800,000 tons per year of solid waste. Since that time, plans to build a plant to burn garbage and produce steam energy have progressed almost to the implementation stage. In addition, METRO is in the process of siting and placing into operation a new landfill site as well as recycling centers and transfer stations. A comprehensive Waste Reduction Plan was formulated and adopted in 1980. Also in 1980, METRO assumed operational control of the City of Portland's landfill.

The majority of solid waste is currently disposed of in landfills, which is a waste of potential energy and recyclable resources. Solid waste disposal cannot be adequately addressed at just the local level. Public education on the issues of recycling, resource recovery, and waste reduction is needed. The franchising of disposal sites is viewed as beneficial; however, the lack of a franchised collection system has hindered efforts of curb-side recycling, disposal of yard debris, et cetera. The siting of regional landfills is becoming a major difficulty, and there is need of a mechanism for the override of local vetoes of landfill sites.

EVALUATION OF THE METRO EXPERIMENT

After two and one-half years of operation, some drawbacks and disadvantages of the new form of regional governance have emerged. The following presents a brief evaluation of the operation of METRO.

The creation of METRO was an intellectual enterprise and not the result of an obvious service breakdown or governmental crisis. This impetus has left METRO without a broad constituency or a particular, pressing, visible problem to solve through which legitimacy can be gained. Consequently, METRO has involved itself in a number of areas to try to demonstrate its usefulness; at least one of these attempts has backfired and created some strong animosities against METRO. METRO's current chance to gain legitimacy is in the solid waste area in which success in the areas of siting of a new landfill and construction of the resource recovery facility are prerequisites to the agency's gaining favorable public support.

Based in part upon the lack of constituency cited above, and in part on the elected council and executive officer feature of METRO, there has been a tendancy to make agency operations overly political. At times, this situation has been manifested in political struggles between the council and executive officer. More often, however, it appears through the posturing of elected officials in either avoiding or diluting the agency's impact in solving regional problems at the expense of special interest groups. The desire of the elected officials to be popular in the short term, as opposed to making tough, long-term decisions, has tended to cause a lack of resolve and follow-through in some of the development issue areas the agency was formed to address. Perhaps what is needed to offset this trend is a strong citizen group, like the Citizens' League in Minneapolis, which could serve as a watchdog and foil when the institution's politics override regional interests.

The fact that Clark County, Washington, is not a participating member of METRO has led to an unfortunate severing of metropolitan policy development. While approximately one-third of the region's growth will occur in Clark County, only narrow *ad hoc* functional agreements exist to coordinate efforts with METRO. The situation has so deteriorated from the former arrangements under CRAG that Clark County formed its own separate MPO for transportation planning. Although provisions for liaison and committee participation are actively pursued, the lack of joint policy development, and in some cases, intra-area competition, have hurt the efficient operation of the metropolitan area.

The goal of the Tri-County Citizens' Commission to bring accountability into regional decision making has been achieved in the current institutional form. The accountability factor has been driven home through elections, court decisions, and actions of citizen special-interest groups. The mere fact that a separate, directly elected policy body exists provides more press coverage and, therefore, more public understanding of the regional concept. The accountability extends to regional decisions not made as well as to those that are made.

The independence of METRO has established a vehicle for

expression and enforcement of a regional perspective. At various times during its existence, METRO has been able to establish regional policies, such as regional housing mix and densities, on a uniform basis that would not be possible under the traditional voluntary council of governments structure. Similarly, on several occasions, METRO has had to litigate individual local jurisdictions' planning and development decisions in order to preserve regional equity. The ability to deal with local jurisdictions on an equal basis has brought into focus the trade-offs and interrelationships between regional and local jurisdictions' governance issues.

METRO's enabling legislation provides a model set of powers to take the initial steps necessary to establish a metropolitan government. Now the major threat to METRO's independence is the lack of a stable financial base. On the whole, exposure to a strong, independent, regional entity has resulted in increased cognizance and acceptance of considering regional interest in making local governance decisions.

The long-term goal of the founders of METRO was to have it assume all but the judicial functions of the counties, thereby reducing the three-tiered local government system to a two-tiered system. The enabling legislation provided a shell or a framework for such an evolution and set out a recommended sequence for merging single-purpose regional agencies into an accountable system of regional governance. This popularly ratified base has made it possible for METRO to influence the provision and timing of a variety of public services and be invited to participate in a number of local government decision processes to achieve recognition and implementation of previously developed regional plans.

METRO'S FUTURE

While METRO will not be able to achieve as much as its founders envisioned in the near future, the strength of its base, coupled with some visible successes in publicly perceived high-priority areas, will establish METRO as a multipurpose, accountable regional agency. It is not foreseeable that it will replace the counties operating in the Portland area or become a general-purpose government. It will, however, provide vital services and a needed perspective to assure that the metropolitan area's outstanding quality of life is maintained, if the public elects dedicated regionalists to METRO'S elective offices.

12. Regional Planning Council Reform in Florida

Nancy E. Stroud

INTRODUCTION

Florida's regional planning councils, through a combination of foresight and fortune, have recently been reaffirmed as important partners in the state planning and management network. Reform in the structure and role of the regional councils was a result of the foresight of state leaders, particularly the governor, to use the councils to help plan for the increase in populaton which by 1990 will make Florida the fourth most populous state in the nation. The fortune in the changes is that they anticipated the shift in federalism which now has regional planning councils nationwide facing a kind of "regional Darwinism," or survival of the fittest. The alliance that is being forged between the state and regional councils in Florida is a kind of fitness program that can help the councils to survive. The changes, in fact, track recommendations made in 1973 by the Advisory Commission on Intergovernmental Relations (ACIR). Added to the unique planning laws of Florida, including the Development of Regional Impact (DRI) provision of the state's land management law, and to the commitment from the governor to use and support the councils, the changes should strengthen the planning and management capacity of the state in the next decade.

141

Florida's population today is about ten million people, an increase of more than 40 percent since 1970 (Florida Office of Planning and Budgeting, 1981). By 1990, the population should approach 13 million. It is expected that Florida will continue to grow twice as fast as other Sun Belt states and more than three times the national average. Most of the new residents will be from out of state, and most will be concentrated along the southern coastlines and the central, citrus-producing area of the state. Florida, whose sun, sand, and surf have been greatly responsible for its growth, has been described as two coasts, back to back. In light of Florida's special environment, and as one of his first actions after being elected governor, Bob Graham appointed a "blue ribbon" citizens committee to review the state resource management laws and their administration for any needed improvements.[1] The Resource Management Task Force deliberated for a year about such issues as agricultural lands preservation, coastal management, water resources, and state, regional, and local planning relationships. In January 1980, the Task Force completed its recommendations, which included a commitment to a major regional role in resource management. The Final Report stated

> Regional management continues as a fragmented and virtually invisible means of influencing resource decisions . . . recommendations urge that the regional agencies be given policy guidance, their activities be integrated, and that they have greater ability to effectively implement management strategies (Resource Management Task Force, 1980, pp. 3, 8).

THE REGIONAL PLANNING SYSTEM

The Task Force recommendations helped to set the agenda for the Graham administration in the following legislative session. The governor gave particular support to the two sets of recommendations regarding regional planning, and most of the recommendations for statutory change were enacted in the 1980 session. The first set of recommendations was a series of reforms to the DRI process; the second set restructured and strengthened the state system of regional planning councils. Since that time, progress in implementing the changes has had its fits and starts, influenced both by the changing political winds and the governmental inertia that haunts the bureaucratic halls and makes governmental change extremely difficult.

The DRI process itself has contributed significantly to the stature of Florida's regional planning councils, and was in fact the impetus for organizing many of the councils in the first place in the early 1970s. The DRI process, established in the Florida Environmental Land and Water Management Act of 1972 requires certain large developments to undergo review by designated regional agencies in regard to development impacts on the region. Specifically, regional agencies must assess whether

1. The development will have a favorable or unfavorable impact on the environmental and natural resources in the region;
2. The development will have a favorable or unfavorable impact on the economy of the region;
3. The development will efficiently use or unduly burden water, sewer, solid waste disposal, or other necessary public facilities;
4. The development will efficiently use or unduly burden transportation facilities;
5. The development will favorably or adversely affect the ability of people to find adequate housing reasonably accessible to their places of employment; and
6. The development complies or does not comply with such other criteria for determining regional impact as the regional planning agency shall deem as appropriate.

The regional review must be considered by the local government when awarding a local development permit for the project, as must local land development regulations and any adopted state land development plan applicable to the area. The regional agency may appeal a local government decision regarding a DRI to the governor and the cabinet. In turn, the governor and the cabinet may then approve or disapprove the local development order with conditions.

REFORM IMPLEMENTATION

The DRI process captures for state and regional review a significant number of projects that will shape the future landscape of Florida. In the first five years of the program, 1973–78, regional
agencies reviewed 257 DRI applications, 75 percent of which were
residential developments (Florida Division of State Planning,
1978). Dwelling units involved in these DRI applications ranged
from almost 700,000 units in the first year, to a low point in
1976–77 of 26,171 dwelling units. Other types of developments
that were reviewed in the first five years include 32 shopping centers, 13 transmission lines, ten amusement and recreational facilities, 13 mines, 11 office parks, eight ports, eight petroleum storage
facilities, four schools, four airports, four industrial plants, and one
hospital. During the same time, the state land planning agency issued binding determinations on 279 projects in regard to their status as DRI's, and 308 determinations of the applicability of vested
rights on proposed projects. Since 1978, 89 DRI applications have
been filed, as have more than 150 binding letters on DRI status.[2]
It should be remembered that the projects that undergo DRI review are large-scale projects involving, for example, 3000 or more
residential units in populous counties and 250 or more units in
rural counties, or shopping centers occupying more than 40 acres
of land. Thus, a considerable amount of new development has
undergone DRI review since the process first began.

 Florida regional planning councils play a significant role in this
unique and important development process. The regional agencies
contribute professional expertise to the review process, assisting
local governments in their review and often influencing the conditions on development that may be attached by the local government
to local development orders. This regional advisory role, however,
is further extended as a result of the ability of the regional council
to appeal the subsequent local decision to the governor and cabinet
for review and permit. Because delays through appeal can also increase the financial pressure on the developer, and thus the political pressure on the community, the regional councils have acquired
a stature of notoriety uncommon to the traditional Councils of
Government nationwide.

 Under the statute that established the DRI process, the governor
may designate any regional agency to conduct DRI reviews. A key
decision was made in the first year of the process to use regional

planning councils, as opposed to other regional agencies, for that review. At that time, in 1972, only five multicounty councils were active in Florida, with membership of less than half of the counties in the state. However, state growth management concerns exploded in that same period, resulting in the passage of a number of state planning, water resource management, and land management laws in addition to that which established the DRI process. The State Comprehensive Planning Act of 1972, among other provisions, enabled the state planning office to administratively establish substate planning districts to aid in state planning efforts. The state did establish eleven substate districts in the early 1970s and designated a regional planning council for each district. Membership in the councils is voluntary, but by 1980 all but two counties were members of a regional council. Nevertheless, counties are automatically included in the coverage of the established councils for state-mandated activities, such as DRI review.

Despite the early linkage of the regional councils and the DRI process, there has been a continuing debate over the years about whether other regional or state agencies with greater financial and professional resources should be designated as the DRI review agencies. The Resource Management Task Force considered such a transfer but concluded that the regional planning councils were the most appropriate agencies for the comprehensive review that the DRI process entails. However, the Task Force also concluded that it was necessary for the councils to be strengthened in their capacities to reflect regional concerns, as opposed to the constituent local governments of which they were formed, and thus tied the retention of the DRI review to reform of the regional councils. The Task Force went on to recommend, and the legislature passed, amendments to streamline the DRI process, improve oversight, and allow the process to be used for coordinated permitting. In so amending the DRI legislation, the state reaffirmed the value of this unique planning and permitting tool, a political victory for planning that in itself is significant for future land use in Florida.

The Regional Planning Council Act of 1980 is the second major legislative enactment implementing the Task Force recommendations directly relevant to regional councils. The legislation enhances the planning and coordinating abilities of the regional planning councils by requiring three major changes. First, council boards must include gubernatorial appointees of one-third of their membership. Second, councils must adopt regional comprehensive policy plans to be used as standards for state-mandated activities, including the DRI process. Finally, the councils are now organized essentially under one enabling statute and are required to adopt procedural rules that are consistent throughout the state for the conduct of state activities. The implementation of these changes so far, and the future possibilities are discussed below.

REGIONAL COUNCIL ORGANIZATION

One constant criticism of regional councils in Florida, and indeed throughout the nation, is that the councils, composed of local elected officials, cannot achieve local consensus on regional issues, but rather act as forums for trading of local concerns. Florida councils have been restructured so that one-third of the membership of the board must be appointed by the governor, with the remaining two-thirds elected local officials. It was expected that these appointments would enable persons to serve who had a more clearly regional perspective, without primary ties to particular localities. The implementation of the new membership requirements has gone beyond that initial objective. Governor Graham has made it a practice to appoint to each council a member who serves concurrently by his appointment on a regional water management district. In this way, the two major regional resource agencies in the state have potential for improved communication and cooperation. Furthermore, a partnership with the water management district is a distinct advantage to the regional councils.

Five water management districts have been established in Florida under the Water Resources Act of 1972. The district's major responsibility is to permit for water consumption and surface water management, and they also must develop regional water plans. Boards are appointed by the governor, and they have *ad valorem* taxing powers. Therefore, resources available to the district and the powers of the district exceed that of the planning councils considerably. The more that regional councils can collaborate with the districts in planning and project review, the better use can be made of limited financial resources. From a planning perspective, the relationship between land and water management in Florida is tightly interwoven and thus also well served by collaborative planning. The governor has also made a practice of appointing the more than 100 new council members from diverse backgrounds, including planners, developers, environmentalists, academicians, lawyers, and business representatives. A strong effort has also been made to appoint women and minorities to the regional councils. The consensus from the regional council directors in 1981 is that the general quality of the appointments has exceeded their expectations and are indeed a welcome addition to the boards.

Previous to the 1980 act, the councils had a choice of two statutes under which to organize and maximum freedom to adopt organizational rules. Now, in order to carry out state-mandated functions such as the DRI process, the councils must be organized under the new law and under common state standards for membership and organizational rules. Following the 1980 legislation, all councils were reorganized under the new act. Under the close supervision of the state, better representation according to population on the councils was generally achieved, including representation of member cities as well as member counties. State guidelines also required that gubernatorial appointees be represented by one-third of the membership of executive boards.

Perhaps the most difficult of the new reforms to implement has been the requirement that the regional planning councils develop comprehensive regional policy plans. Under the law, the plans must be approved by the governor and adopted by the councils by formal administrative rule. The plans, upon adoption, become the standards for regional functions such as review of state-mandated local government comprehensive plans and developments of regional impact. The law provides also that the plans of the councils are to be consistent with those of the water management districts, with disputes over inconsistencies in the plans to be resolved by the governor and cabinet. The importance assigned to the planning process is indicated by these legislative mandates. Adoption by rule gives the plans the status of law; coordination with water plans are compelled and made accountable to the state; and the governor, as chief state planning officer, has approval power over the regional plans.

In fact, the regional plans have become the key links in an evolving state-integrated policy framework, and are perceived as such by the governor (Graham, 1981). As part of that framework, the Governor's Office is developing state policy guidelines to be used in the approval of the regional plans. The effort to develop state guidelines has not been a smooth one, particularly as the Office of Planning and Budgeting and the Department of Veteran and Community Affairs have attempted to sort out their respective responsibilities. However, the governor has directed that guidelines be prepared by March 1982, with responsibility for assuring that the deadline be met assigned to the Office of Planning and Budgeting.

EVALUATION

The regional councils themselves initially responded well to the need for comprehensive plans, although they have tied their performance to the state ability to provide plan development funds. Executive directors in early 1981 agreed on a common format and methodology for preparing the plans as preparation for a report to the legislature and request for funding. Enthusiasm has waned since the 1981 state legislative session refused to fund their approximately $4 million request, or the governor's $2 million budget for planning. Since 1974, the councils have been funded at about $500,000 annually, and such funds were continued for 1980-81. Additional funds were provided to begin hurricane and disaster plans, and to be used as a kind of test by the legislature of the planning capability of the councils.

The legislative concern for budget constraints, rather than a disregard for the new legislation, is primarily responsible for the reluctance to fund new planning. A sales tax increase, the only realistic source of new state revenue, failed to be enacted in the 1980 legislature in the midst of extraordinary political infighting. Against the background of Florida's relatively low property tax, lack of income tax, and 4 percent sales tax, prospects for revenue increases in 1982 seem hopeful, but far from certain. At the same time, the reluctance of the regional planning councils to go forward with regional planning without greatly increased funding is an irony and, according to some observers, a political miscalculation. Thus, the ideologies of fiscal conservatism that have trickled down from Washington, in addition to the ordinary difficulties in government agencies, leave Florida teetering on the brink of successful regional management.

Florida has taken significant steps to modernize its regional councils along the lines of the 1973 ACIR recommendations, which included provision of state legal authority for areawide organizations, gubernatorial appointments, and the strengthening of the regional policy role (ACIR, 1973). Other ACIR recommendations, also made by the governor's Resource Management Task Force, remain an unfinished agenda. These include mandatory county membership, review and consolidation of other substate regional agency boundaries, and stabilized, increased funding for the councils. The future holds possibilities for these changes, as well as others recommended by the Office of Planning and Budgeting. For example, the Office of Planning and Budgeting has expressed interest in the use of regional plans for the development of the state budget, particularly in state capital improvements programming. The governor is also interested in giving the councils a greater role in state facility siting.

These and other reforms will probably be necessary for the long-term survival of regional planning councils everywhere, as the federal monies that have created and propped up regional councils during the last decade disappear (DeGrove and Stroud, 1981). Like Florida regional planning councils, Councils of Governments nationwide will have to ally more closely with their states to survive the federal cutbacks in financial and program responsibilities. Councils should be turning to their states to provide assistance in planning and budget allocation services to the state. States may turn to their substate agencies for these services, particularly if true block grants to states become a federal mode of operation. Further, regions will be better fit to survive if they begin to provide more direct services to local and regional areas. This may be aided by functional consolidation moves from local government agencies to regional agencies, necessitated by fiscal conservatism. Consolidation of regional agencies or at least closer coordination through shared staff or board members may be another successful survival technique now being tested in Florida.

CONCLUSION

Governor Graham predicted in 1980 that "Florida will continue to grow but it will be increasingly politically isolated because the constituency for growth in the South will be small in Washington" (Graham, 1981). Federal cuts not only in the federal planning programs, but also in programs such as road and sewer subsidies, will adversely affect Southern growth states, and Florida particularly. Graham went on to say,

Whether Florida meets its growth needs effectively, efficiently, and with farsighted cooperation; or poorly, wastefully, and through adverse parochialism, depends to a large extent on regional (agencies) . . . A regional approach to resource management is a necessity.

The response of the regional agencies could fulfill either of the governor's scenarios. A survey conducted by the University of Florida's Department of Urban and Regional Planning in the spring of 1981, indicates that both executive directors and chairpersons of the councils believe that

1. State agencies will be much more responsive to the councils;
2. The state will use regional councils as vehicles for state planning and program implementation;
3. There appears to be a strengthening constituency for regional planning; and
4. The required regional plan will have a significant impact on the future growth of the several regions in Florida (Starnes, 1981).

Such responses indicate that the state commitment to regional planning is perceived as genuine and the regions have high hopes for the new alliance between the state and regional agencies. It remains to be seen whether or not the councils will rise to the challenge. With the continued commitment from the governor, which seems assured, and the blessing of the legislature in the form of increased funding, which seems less certain, these hopes may be realized in the near future.

PART FIVE

Conclusion

13. The Prospects for Regional Planning

Charles R. Warren

INTRODUCTION

The United States has had a long and varied experience with regional planning at various levels of governmental hierarchy. A form of regionalism has been a part of the American system of governance since early in the Twentieth Century. Regional planning has been inspired by civic and voluntary groups, carried out by the collective action of local governments, established and supported by state government, and, during the past 25 years, encouraged and funded by agencies of the federal government. As a result, by the 1970s, regional planning agencies operated in virtually every metropolitan and rural area of the United States.

Given the long evolution of regional planning and the widespread existence of regional agencies, regionalism seemed to be an assured feature of the governmental system. However, the recent budget cuts by the Reagan Administration and the New Federalism proposal appear to have significant impact on regional planning agencies. These agencies which have been supported by the federal government over the last 20 years are likely to experience substantial withdrawal of funding from the federal government.

Federal financial support for regional planning has constituted, on the average, 76 percent of the budgets of generalist regional councils and 92 percent of specialized regional agencies. A recent survey of the federal budget reductions indicates about one-third of the 39 programs supporting multicounty substate activities had ceased operation by the start of Fiscal 1982. It also shows that only about one-half of the 39 programs are likely to survive in some form into Fiscal 1983 (Reid and Stam, 1982). Many of those surviving programs will be forced into major transformation of structure. The impact of the budget reductions in these programs will have significant effect on regional planning agencies. Many regional planning agencies are now undergoing restructuring through cuts in both staffing and activity levels. It appears that the average regional council will experience a reduction of 40 to 50 percent of federal funding. It seems likely that some of the existing regional planning agencies will have to discontinue their operation due to the federal budget cuts.

Despite declining federal financial support in the coming years, the possibility of greater responsibility for state governments may provide new opportunity for state-level and substate regional planning activities.[1] The New Federalism initiatives have led to a major transition in the history of regional planning. Regional agencies are now facing a difficult period of reappraisal with respect to their purpose, their sources of funding, and the constituencies they serve.

The papers in this volume have assessed the history of regional planning and have provided insights into the prospects for its future. The authors offer a variety of perspectives and experience. The practice of regional planning at different levels of government in a number of states and metropolitan areas have been discussed. This concluding chapter summarizes the findings and insights of the papers and discusses the prospects for regional planning in the coming years.

PERSPECTIVES ON REGIONAL PLANNING

Cassella has presented a well-drawn history of regional planning and governance in the United States. The concept of regionalism has been with us for a long time. Cassella's chronicle begins in 1909 when the National Municipal League called for a "metropolitan district" form of government. The ensuing seven decades show a strong continuity in the problems, needs, and issues surrounding regional planning. The continuing issue has been jurisdictional fragmentation, i.e., a mismatch between political boundary lines and appropriate geographical units for providing public services. While regionalism was advocated by good government groups, no single approach or solution was available for the nation's metropolitan areas, and the logic of regionalism was more often than not overwhelmed by politics and "suburbanitis." These lessons were learned, in the 1940s and 1950s, yet during that period and on into the 1960s commissions and studies on metropolitan problems proliferated. While results disillusioned reformers, national attention was brought to the issue of regional planning and the council of Governments (COGs) movement was launched. Yet, as Cassella admits, "Some of us who were participants and observers in this development saw it as a mixed blessing."

Mogulof, an astute observer of the metropolitan scene, reached the same conclusion in 1971. He warned, however, that the halfway character of COGs may forestall more significant reform (Mogulof, 1971). To some extent, the COGs were empty vessels entrusted with broad and general responsibilities but little authority. Their advisory character and emphasis on planning ensured a weakened role. Cassella reminds us that the National Municipal League stated these prophetic words in 1930: "But to be of value plans must be executed." Cassella proposes that states take a more active role to deal with regional planning issues. He argues that the adjustments in intergovernmental relations are an integral part of the future success of regional planning.

McDowell describes in greater detail the roles of the federal government in the expansion of regional planning in past decades. Now a contraction of federal support is taking place. While in the past, regional agencies served largely as agents of the federal bureaucracy, President Reagan has concluded, in McDowell's words, "that the type of planning done with these funds is that for which the subnational units of government have responsibility; they should, therefore, provide the funding for it." How then do we assess the federal contribution to regional planning as it was carried out over the past three decades? As both Cassella and McDowell point out, regionalism was part of American government long before the national bureaucracy became involved. Yet, there is no doubt that federal funds and requirements made regional planning much more pervasive and helped to institutionalize it in places where it might never have developed. Federal funding enabled regional agenices to attract high quality staff members who in turn provided much needed technical aid to local governments. Inter-local coordination has increased. The A-95 Review Process resulted in less duplication in project funding and, doubtlessly, has saved money.

On the other hand, federal support of regional planning has had its costs. Federal regionalism has been sometimes schizophrenic and contradictory. While it supported comprehensive planning and regional agencies with a generalist perspective, at the same time, it spawned a host of single purpose substate bodies whose allegiances were to functions instead of to governments.

The real test of the federal contribution to regional planning will come in the next few years. Will state and local governments continue to rely on and support regional planning? The response of state governments is critical. The current changes in American federalism dictate a decreased role by the federal government in supporting domestic programs. This is accompanied by expanded responsibilities of state governments for these domestic programs in general and regional planning issues in particular. There are some hopeful signs that the states may respond. These signs will be discussed later.

FUNCTIONAL AREAS OF REGIONAL PLANNING

Politics intrudes into the seemingly pristine world of planning in the area of solid waste management. Holland relates the frustrating tale of trying to plan and implement a badly needed resource re-covery facility in the Cuyahoga County area of Ohio. The solid waste disposal problem was clear and urgent and a regional ap-proach was the obvious and only logical answer. Yet, as Holland related, it did not happen for a number of reasons. First, there was confusion over the responsibility for planning and implementation. Second, the federal government shifted its support from planning to implementation and vacillated on the designation of the regional agency. There was the debilitating effect of local politics. In this case, federal support of regional planning appeared to be harmful. It is apparent from Holland's paper that there is an essential need for an intergovernmental umpire; if the federal government will not play that role, then state government must.

McLellan and Boxer's paper describes the development of coastal zone management in the United States. They go on to discuss some of the problems associated with the integration of natural resources management with the political process involved in the field of coastal management. The authors describe the plight of the planner attempting to work objectively in an environment of shifting goals, changing consensus, and conflicting objectives. The major obejctives, they note, are to "protect and to develop," and those goals are often incompatible. McLellan and Boxer conclude with a look to the future and express cautious optimism that the coastal management process is entrenched deeply enough that the current reductions in federal support will not remove this nationwide program of regional land-use planning from the governmental landscape.

The conflict between government planning and marketplace decision making is raised by Vaughan in his paper on economic development. While admitting that he has erected a "straw-man" planner, Vaughan concludes that traditional planning has little to offer the economic policy maker. In his opinion, planning is too inflexible, unable to comprehend the dynamics of economic systems, and too removed from the operational side of policies and programs. Vaughan's prescription is for planners to become policy analysts and to develop the substantive knowledge of economics, finance, and human resource development that will enable them to recognize when public intervention is warranted and has any possibility of payoff. Finally, Vaughan would merge planning agencies with operating agencies. In his opinion planning will survive only when it is needed, useful, and is supported by a local constituency.

Boyd describes the growth and decline in the federal role in regional planning with respect to the functional area of health care. Boyd traces the evolution of health care from a matter of local concern to an issue of national purpose, and charts the growth of health planning to its maturity as an important tool in resource allocation. He explains that health planning became a system that worked well when it was tied to "health communities" and linked to the "pivotal power of state government." But then federal intrusion and federal definition of "community" began to erode the system. There is the sense that health planning was affordable and a valuable aid in the allocation of resources, yet when resources became scarce, its value was diminished. If federal support for regional health planning ends, the spectre of competition in the marketplace as an alternative to government planning becomes an important issue. Boyd concludes that "The future of health planning lies, at least for the short term, with state governments."

Page focuses both on transportation planning and regional transportation finance, which as he explained, are two very distinct issues. Transportation planning, according to federal law, is to be "comprehensive, cooperative, and continuing," but since the funding sources were largely restricted for highway projects, little remained for transportation planning beyond that single mode. Thus, the "3-C" goals were seldom realized. In order to escape the highway dominance, mass transit planning and financing evolved separately. A further separation has occurred in metropolitan transportation since the planning function was often vested in COGs while operations normally resided in independent public authorities. Page raises the fundamental question, "Should the regional ransportation planning responsibility be divorced from the financial decision-making process?" Again, we see the central issue of the relationship of planning to implementation. Page concludes that public transit is a governmental service, and "It cannot, will not, and should not be self-supporting." The answer, of course, is to subsidize the farebox. Yet, this means that some form of multijurisdictional, dedicated revenue source is required. As difficult as regional planning is, taxation across governmental boundaries is the ultimate test of regionalism. Page presents a type of regionalism that is pervasive and is not simply involved in planning; it is a regional authority which operates programs and delivers public services.

REGIONAL PLANNING AGENCIES

Case studies of four regional agencies are presented, two of which represent the most advanced forms of regionalism in this nation, what might be termed the "regional superstars." A third portrays a regional planning body on the brink of extinction, and the last provides a ray of hope in depicting the emergence of a strong statewide system of regional councils supported by state government. Each case demonstrates the importance of the state role.

Kolderie describes the major contribution that the Twin Cities Metropolitan Council has made to regionalism and governmental theory. This contribution is not only in its precedence, since it was the first independent and authoritative regional body in a major metropolitan area, but in the character of its conception. As

Kolderie explains, two essential principles lie behind the success of the council: first, "It was an action by the state, not by local government," and second, "It was built for the purpose of making policy and political decisions rather than for the operation and administration of a program." The first principle is essential to the second one; the Council has its own political base.

The most important contribution that the Twin Cities has made is an answer to the debate over the relationship between planning and implementation. While the two appear to be divorced in this case, upon closer examination and redefinition of implementation, they are not. The Twin Cities Council makes plans and sets policies, but it also decides; it does not administer. Perhaps this is the appropriate link between planning and implementation. Yet, one wonders how transferable the Minnesota experience is. Few areas, except perhaps Portland, Oregon, are as homogeneous and progressive as Minneapolis-St. Paul. Based on the experience of solid waste planning in Cleveland, it is doubtful that a metropolis of that ilk would embrace such a powerful institution at the regional level.

The tri-state region around New York City provides perhaps the sternest and most unforgiving test for regional planning; the statistics of that region make this case—three states, 27 counties, 600 localities, and 8,000 square miles with 18 million inhabitants. The problem of interstate metropolitan areas has always vexed regional advocates, and is most often ignored. Planning across state boundaries, as well as across local boundaries, further complicates the politics of regionalism. As Reed explains, the Tri-State Regional Planning Commission lacked autonomy and while it depended on the states for resources and policy direction, it was 75 percent federally funded. As such, it found itself in the position of a federal agent whose major purpose is to prepare the required plans. Tri-State was particularly vulnerable to the federal cutbacks and has already reduced its staff size from 277 to 100 employees. The Governors' Task Force on the Future of the Tri-State Regional Planning Commission presented a pessimistic view of the role of the commission in the years to come. It seems quite likely that the commission may be completely dismantled.

The Metropolitan Service District (METRO) of Portland, Oregon, is exactly the kind of body that was envisioned by the National Municipal League in 1909. METRO is a directly elected regional government with multifunctional responsibilities. It came to be after a long history of reform efforts and the final emergence of a public consensus on the need for a new form of regionalism. It represents a civic demand for accountability at the regional level, and reflects a belief in that region that public officials serve best under the electoral process. METRO has strong land-use powers, a broad potential for service delivery, and very tenuous financing, at least for the short term. It is, in short, a very desirable vehicle for regional action, which in the opinion of Kent, requires a grass-roots constituency and possibly a public crisis to reach its potential.

There is a basis for optimism for regional planning because of recent developments in one of our largest and fastest growing states, Florida. Stroud observes that Regional Planning Councils in Florida have become important partners in state planning and management. The Florida legislature in 1980, through statute, transformed its voluntary and advisory regional planning councils into strong, policy-making instruments. Nearly all local governments are now members of a regional council and mandatory membership is being considered, regional policies are required, and the Governor now appoints one-third of the members of each of the eleven regional councils. One may suspect that the state leadership recognized that its revolving framework of laws and regulations to protect Florida's fragile environment, manage its land, and conserve its scarce water had simply outstripped the regional and local institutional capacity. Structural modernization was the only path to policy implementation. Overall, the development of regional councils in Florida presents a possibility for effective regional planning activities under state initiative.

ISSUES AND PROSPECTS

The collection of papers in this volume has raised a number of fundamental questions about the viability and future of regional planning. Will support for regional planning be continued? If so, where will it come from: from the federal government, from state government, or from local government? Does the rationale for regional planning need to be reconstructed? How can regional planning be tied more closely to implementation and resource allocation?

Resolution of these issues depends on the type and form of regionalism involved, and the jurisdictional context in which it operates. The responses to the challenges now facing regional planning will vary widely across the country. There will be attrition in the number of regional entities, particularly among those more specialized agencies whose purpose and support is tied to categorical federal assistance programs. There are a large number of regional service delivery authorities which operate water and sewer systems and provide mass transit and other regional services. These functional bodies will continue and may even increase in number. In contrast, generalist regional planning agencies or COGs are clearly at a threshold.

There is a consensus among the authors in this volume that the future of regional planning rests primarily with state government. The continued viability and utility of regionalism does depend upon the interest and support of state government. Yet this conclusion leads us to a number of specific questions about the role of state government. How can regional councils gain state support? Can regional planning contribute to better governance when there are less resources for government? Are regional councils politically useful tools for state government? Can state-initiated regional planning provide a more efficient and equitable use of resources?

It has been arued that greater fiscal austerity will increase, rather than lessen, the need for regional approaches. It can be maintained that the imperative for planning and interlocal cooperation in service delivery will be greater when resources are more scarce. There is enormous duplication of effort and inefficiency in the current intergovernmental system, some of which can be attributed directly to the proliferation and fragmentation of federal aid programs. A shift toward block grants and a reduced role of the federal government in providing domestic programs are giving states and local governments greater discretion and flexibility to set priorities. This situation can serve as the basis upon which to build a new rationale for regional planning.

Current trends in federalism point toward an increasing role for state governments in the financing of state and local services. The growing power of state governments to allocate resources to localities may mean a new role for regional planning agencies. The states will face an imperative to improve their planning and budgeting processes and to set priorities across a broad range of programs and functions. This may, in turn, create pressure for a comparable planning and budgeting process at the substate regional level.

There are precedents for state use of regional agencies to assist in resource allocation. Kentucky has utilized its area development districts to integrate and plan the use of federal and state grants for capital development projects in each region. Minnesota has vested the Twin Cities Council with authority to examine local budgets and to ensure that state investments are consistent with the "Regional Development Framework." There are also emerging examples of regional councils being given a role in the allocation of the small cities Community Development Block Grant.

According to Reed (1981), substate planning districts in Arizona are going to be utilized to allocate funds. Similar roles for regional commissions are being considered in other states such as Texas and Mississippi. There are likely to be instances where regional agencies can serve as political buffers between the states and localities in resolving the allocation of scarce funds. Such a role might not only be politically useful to state leadership, but might also be acceptable to local officials. City and county officials may prefer to divide up the resources among themselves rather than rely on distant state officials to decide for them.

The need to achieve economies of scale in some public services could increase centralization and promote greater use of regional authorities. This prospect may also enhance the potential involvement of regional planning agencies in resource allocation and service delivery. While separate, multijurisdictional authorities which rely largely on user charges are a service delivery alternative which can relieve the pressure on city and county budgets, they can also lead to a proliferation of regional staffs and uncoordinated investments. Regional planning agencies can serve to coordinate and control the activities of independent authorities on behalf of local governments.

The essential linkage between planning and implementation can be achieved through several alternatives. Each of our metropolitan areas contain numerous planning and operating agencies at the substate regional level. Consolidation or merger of these regional agencies is one alternative that could place planning and implementation responsibilities under a single policy body and executive. This is the model being developed in Portland, Oregon. Economies of scale and increased coordination among functional staffs and planners should result from consolidation of regional structures.

A second alternative, short of consolidation, is to grant comprehensive regional planning agencies the authority to exercise policy control over single-purpose regional bodies such as those involved in water, sewage, and transportation. Budgetary review and approval over capital investments made by functional agencies in a region may become a necessity if the infrastructure needs are to be met in the context of scarce public resources. The Twin Cities

Council has taken this approach; other regions may need to follow suit.

A third alternative is to make regional planning an integral component of the state planning and budgetary process. Regional councils could serve as effective brokers or "middlemen" in state relations with local governments. They could articulate local needs, transmit state policies, and reconcile statewide priorities with a region's interests. To do so, they must be provided with funding and delegated authority by the governor and legislature. Florida has moved in this direction; Georgia and Kentucky have also used their substate districts to some extent in this way. Federal devolution to the state governments might well provide a further impetus to the adoption of this model.

While the future of regional planning may appear bleak in the short term because of dramatic and sudden shifts in the federal role, prospects over the long term are more sanguine. There is a continuity and history of regionalism in the United States that spans at least seven decades; a process of institutionalization that is not likely to be reversed or ended. There is a logic and practical necessity for regional arrangements, and while this may be frustrated by politics and parochialism, it cannot be ignored. We need to recognize that the American system of government is highly dynamic. The adaptation and evolution of our governing institutions is a continuing process. While the future shape of regionalism may seem uncertain, there are good prospects that regional planning will continue to play an important role in our system of government.

Notes

CHAPTER 1

1. For example, the Governors' Task Force on the Future of the Tri-State Regional Planning Commission was organized in 1979 "for the purpose of examining the mission and structure of the Tri-State Regional Planning Commission, recommending changes that would better enable the Commission to meet the planning needs of the future, and assisting, as directed by the governors, in the implementation of those changes." See Governors' Task Force on the Future of the Tri-State Regional Planning Commission (1981).

2. The proposal was made by *America's New Beginning: A Program for Economic Recovery* (1981). For more detailed accounts of the federal budget reduction, see Nathan (1981).

3. Amendment X of the U.S. Constitution says, "The Powers not delegated to the United States by the Constitution, nor prohibited by it to the States, are reserved to the States, respectively, or to the people."

4. Danielson, Hershey and Bayne (1977) note that state and local governments have remained significant due to the diffusion of governmental responsibilities accompanied by political decentralization.

5. Literature on planning has long emphasized the coordinative and feedback function of planning for resource allocation. See, for example, Branch (1950) and Meyerson (1956).

6. A document prepared by the American Institute of Planners in 1962 defines "metropolitan planning" as follows: it is "comprehensive planning applied to areas containing a large urban concentration where dominant economic, social, and physical factors may over-arch local and even State boundaries. The function of metropolitan planning is to contribute to the formulation and implementation of optimal public policy for the metropolitan area." See American Institute of Planners (1962).

7. For a description and analysis of these agencies, see Derthick (1974).

8. When Propostion 13 was passed, regional planning agencies in California, such as the Association of Bay Area Governments (ABAG), had to reduce the size of their operation.

CHAPTER 3

1. The views expressed in this paper do not necessarily represent those of the Advisory Commission on Intergovernmental Relations.

2. The number of interstate metropolitan areas has been set tentatively at 41 following the 1980 Census population count. Accounting for the fact that some of these are within larger "consolidated" metropolitan areas, there are 39 interstate areas of contiguous urbanization. After the 1980 data on commuting patterns have been analyzed, these numbers may change slightly (U.S. Office of Management and Budget, 1981).

CHAPTER 4

1. Mayor George V. Voinovich was re-elected to a four-year term on November 3, 1981, with over 75 percent of the vote cast.

CHAPTER 5

1. The following discussion is drawn in part from Knecht (1979).

CHAPTER 6

1. The views expressed are those of the author and do not reflect the views of the Office of Development Planning or the State of New York.

2. At the time of writing, it appears that all of HUD's 701 planning grants, EDA's 302 planning grants, and a part of the Appalachian Regional Commission's planning money will disappear. There may be some additional funds available from state governments—at their discretion from the Small City Block Grant program.

3. See Wilson, (1981). Here Wilson provides several examples, both good and bad, of how academic disciplines have helped change the context of public policy discussions. A good example is the idea of education vouchers, first ridiculed in the early 1960s, and now seriously considered as part of a replacement to the Comprehensive Employment and Training Act (CETA) program.

4. For adminstrative changes in programs that require no legislation or expenditure, the process does not have to be governed by the annual legislative or budget cycle.

CHAPTER 8

1. Testimony by American Public Transit Association, July 15, 1981, U.S. House Committee on Public Works.

CHAPTER 9

1. In remarks at a conference on urban problems at the Academy for Contemporary Problems, Columbus, Ohio, 1973.

2. The emergence of a health-care 'marketplace' in the Twin Cities area is closely followed, and promoted, by a locally based health policy institute, InterStudy. The council/health board turned down a proposal from a major local multihospital group, Fairview Community Hospitals, for a 150-bed hospital in the southern suburbs, in 1980. In 1981, however, with a new chairman and 10 new members, the board approved a second application.

3. Conversation with Harold Horn, director, Cable Television Information Center, Washington, D.C.

4. The best explanation, by far, of the so-called "fiscal disparities" act is in Gilje (1977). The most recent calculation of the current situation is in Gilje (1980).

5. In June 1978, York University, Toronto, convened a meeting on urban development and governance. Representatives from the Twin Cities area were included. Speakers from Toronto expressed considerable admiration for the Metropolitan Council, which, in contrast to their own, is responsible for operational programs, and in which the system of representation, built out of the municipalities in the Toronto region, creates a "delegate" system of voting which makes compromise and decision making difficult. Toronto's system, they said, is very good at doing things and very bad at deciding what is the right thing to do.

6. One good explanation of the private sector/public sector relationship is in "The Good Citizens League Itself," available from the Citizens League, 84 South Sixth Street, Minneapolis, Minnesota 55402.

7. See the testimony of Ted Kolderie on this subject, before the Subcommittee on the City, Committee on Banking, Currence and Urban Affairs, U.S. House of Representatives, April 4, 1977.

CHAPTER 10

1. Transmittal letter to the Governors from Chester Rapkin, Chairman of the Task Force on the Future of the Tri-State Regional Planning Commission.

2. Interview with David Mamman, Deputy Director of the Task Force on the Future of the Tri-State Regional Planning Commission on October 2, 1981.

3. Ibid.

4. Letter from the Task Force to Governors Byrne, O'Neill and Carey.

CHAPTER 11

1. Some people maintain that the ballot title that was selected by the State Legislative Counsel "Abolish CRAG and Reorganize MSD" was the key to the number of positive votes for the issue.

CHAPTER 12

1. The author of this paper served as staff director for the Task Force.
2. Statistics from 1978 to the present are from Howard Pardue, Senior Planner, Bureau of Land and Water Management, Florida Department of Veteran and Community Affairs. Telephone conversation of September 15, 1981.

CHAPTER 13

1. In the State of the Union message delivered in February 1982, President Reagan proposed a transfer of most domestic programs to the states.

References

Abler, Ronald; Adams, John; and Borchert, John (1976). *The Twin Cities of St. Paul and Minneapolis*. Cambridge, Mass.: Ballinger Publishing Co.

Advisory Commission on Intergovernmental Relations (1962). *Factors Affecting Voter Reaction to Governmental Reorganization in Metropolitan Areas*. Report M-15. Washington, D.C.: U.S. Government Printing Office.

—— (1965). *Metropolitan Social and Economic Disparities: Implication for Intergovernmental Relations in Central Cities and Suburbs*. Report A-25. Washington, D.C.: U.S. Government Printing Office.

—— (1966a). *Alternative Approaches to Governmental Reorganization in Metropolitan Areas*. Washington, D.C.: U.S. Government Printing Office.

—— (1966b). *Metropolitan Council of Governments*. Washington, D.C.: U.S. Government Printing Office.

—— (1969). *Urban America and the Federal System: Commission Findings and Proposals*. Report M-47. Washington, D.C.: U.S. Government Printing Office.

—— (1971). *For a More Perfect Union: County Reform*. Report M-61. Washington, D.C.: U.S. Government Printing Office.

—— (1972). *Profits of County Government: An Information Report*. Report M-72. Washington, D.C.: U.S. Government Printing Office.

—— (1973). "Regional Decision Making: New Strategies for Substate Districts." *Substate Regionalism and the Federal System*. Report A-43, Vol. 1 Washington, D.C.: U.S. Government Printing Office.

—— (1973). "Regional Governance: Promise and Performance—Case Studies." *Substate Regionalism and the Federal System*. Report A-41, Vol. 2. Washington, D.C.: U.S. Government Printing Office.

—— (1973). "The Challenge of Local Government Reorganization." *Substate Regionalism and the Federal System*. Report A-44, Vol. 3. Washington, D.C.: U.S. Government Printing Office.

—— (1973). "Governmental Functions and Processes: Local and Area-wide." *Substate Regionalism and the Federal System.* Report A-45, Vol. 4. Washington, D.C.: U.S. Government Printing Office.

—— (1973). "A Look to the North: Canadian Regional Experience." *Substate Regionalism and the Federal System.* Report A-46. Vol. 5. Washington, D.C.: U.S. Government Printing Office.

—— (1973). "Hearings on Substate Regionalism," *Substate Regionalism and the Federal System.* Report A-43a, Vol. 6. Washington, D.C.: U.S. Government Printing Office.

—— (1976). *Improving Urban America: A Challenge to Federalism.* Report M-107. Washington, D.C.: U.S. Government Printing Office.

—— (1977). *Regionalism Revisited: Recent Areawide and Local Responses.* Report A-66. Washington, D.C.: U.S. Government Printing Office.

—— (Forthcoming). *State and Local Roles in the Federal System.* Washington, D.C.: U.S. Government Printing Office.

American Institute of Planners (1962). *The Role of Metropolitan Planning.* American Institute of Planners.

Armstrong, Regina Belz (1980). *Regional Accounts: Structure and Performance of the New York Region's Economy in the Seventies.* Bloomington, Ind.: Indiana University Press.

Aron, Joan B. (1969). *The Quest for Regional Cooperation: A Study of the New York Metropolitan Regional Council.* Berkeley, Cal.: University of California Press.

Association of Bay Area Governments (1970). *Regional Plan 1970–1990.* Berkeley, Cal.: Association of Bay Area Governments.

Baldinger, Stanley (1971). *Planning and Governing the Metropolis: The Twin Cities Experience.* New York, N.Y.: Praeger Publishers.

Banfield, Edward C. (1957). "The Politics of Metropolitan Organization." *Midwest Journal of Political Science.* Vol. 1, No. 1 (May): 77–91.

Banfield, Edward C. and Wilson, James Q. (1963). *City Politics.* New York, N.Y.: Vintage Books.

Baram, Michael S. (1976). *Environmental Law and the Siting of Facilities, Issues in Land Use and Coastal Zone Management.* Cambridge, Mass.: Ballinger Publishing Company.

Barnes, Philip W. (1969). *Metropolitan Coalitions: A Study of Councils of Government in Texas.* Austin, Tex.: Institute of Public Affairs, University of Texas.

Beckman, Norman (1960). "Federal Long-Range Planning: The Heritage of the National Resources Planning Board." *Journal of American Institute of Planners.* Vol. 26, No. 2.

—— (1974). "Federal Policy for Metropolitan Governance." *National Civic Review.* Vol. 63, No. 3.

Bertsch, Berger and Christensen (1980). *Urban Impact Review and A-95 State and Metropolitan Clearinghouses: An Evaluation and Recommendations for the 1980s.* Prepared for the Office of Community Planning and Development, Department of Housing and Urban Development by the Academy for Contemporary Affairs.

Bollens, John C. et al. (1970). *The Metropolis: Its People, Politics and Economic Life.* 2nd ed. New York, N.Y.: Harper and Row.

Booth, David A. (1963). *Metropolitics: The Nashville Consolidation.* East Lansing, Mich.: Institute for Community Development and Services, Michigan State University.

Borchept, John (1961). "The Twin Cities Urbanized Area: Past, Present, Future." *Geograhical Review.* Vol. 51, No. 1.

Bradford, David F. and Oates, Wallace E. (1974). "Suburban Exploitation of Central Cities and Governmental Structure." *Redistribution Through Public Choice.* Edited by Harold M. Hochman and George E. Peterson. Published in cooperation with The Urban Institute, Washington, D.C. New York, N.Y.: Columbia University Press.

Branch, Melville C. (1950). "Concerning Coordinative Planning." *Journal of the American Institute of Planners,* Vol. 16, No. 3.

Bromage, Arthur W. (1962). *Political Representation in Metropolitan Agencies.* Ann Arbor, Mich.: Institute of Public Administration, University of Michigan.

Brown, Willie Jr. (1969). "Regional Government: Impact on the Poor." *Toward a Bay Area Regional Organization.* Edited by Harriet Nathan and Stanley Scott. Berkeley, Cal.: Institute for Governmental Studies, University of California.

Burton, Richard (1971). *On the Relevance of Governmental Reorganization to National Urban Growth Policy.* Working paper. Washington, D.C.: The Urban Institute.

Business Week. (1981). "Watt Tries an End Run on Offshore Oil Leases." (July 20).

Campbell, Alan K. (1977). "Metropolitan Governance and the Mature Metropolis." *The Mature Metropolis.* Edited by Charles L. Leven. Lexington, Mass.: Lexington Books.

Campbell, Alan K., ed. (1970). *The States and the Urban Crisis.* Englewood Cliffs, N.J.: Prentice Hall.

Campbell, Alan K. and Bahl, Roy W., eds. (1976). *State and Local Government: The Political Economy of Reform.* New York, N.Y.: The Free Press.

Carson, Rachel (1962). *Silent Spring.* Greenwich, Conn.: Fawcett Publications.

Carver, Joan (1973). "Responsiveness and Consolidation: A Case Study." *Urban Affairs Quarterly.* Vol. 9, No. 2.

Chamberlain, Stephen P. (1979). "A Petroleum Industry Perspective on Federal Coastal Zone Management Reform." *Coastal Zone Management Journal,* Vol. 6, No. 4.

Chasis, Sarah (1979). "Problem and Prospects of Coastal Zone Management: An Environmental Viewpoint." *Coastal Zone Management Journal,* Vol. 6, No. 4.

—— (1980). "The Coastal Zone Management Act." *Journal of the American Planning Association.* Vol. 46, No. 2.

Cion, Richard M. (1971). "Accommodation Par Excellence: The Lakewood Plan." *Metropolitan Politics: A Reader.* 2nd ed. Edited by Michael N. Danielson. Boston, Mass: Little, Brown and Company.

Citizens League (1967). *A Metropolitan Council for the Twin Cities Area.* Minneapolis, Minn.: The Citizens League.

—— (1980). *Issues of the 80's: Enlarging Our Capacity to Adapt.* Minneapolis, Minn.: The Citizens League.

Committee for Economic Development (1960). *Guiding Local Government.* New York, N.Y.: Committee for Economic Development.

—— (1966). *Modernizing Local Government to Secure a Balanced Federalism.* New York, N.Y.: Committee for Economic Development.

—— (1970). *Reshaping Government in Metropolitan Areas.* New York, N.Y.: Committee for Economic Development.

Costickyan, Edward N. and Lehman, Maxwell (1973). *New Strategies for Regional Cooperation: A Model for the Tri-State New York-New Jersey-Connecticut Area.* New York, N.Y.: Praeger Publishers.

Council on Environmental Quality (1979). *Environmental Quality.* The Tenth Annual Report of the Council on Environmental Quality. Washington, D.C.: U.S. Government Printing Office.

Council of State Governments (1955). *The State and the Metropolitan Problem.* Chicago, Ill.: Council of State Governments.

—— (1962). *State Responsibility in Urban Regional Development: A Report to the Governors' Conference.* Chicago, Ill.: Council of State Governments.

Crecine, John P., ed. (1970). "Financing the Metropolis: Public Policy in Urban Economics." *Urban Affairs Annual Reviews.* Vol. 4. Beverly Hills, Cal.: Sage Publications.

Dade County Metropolitan Study Commission (1971). *Final Report and Recommendations.*

Dahl, Robert (1967). *Who Governs: Democracy and Power in an American City.* New Haven, Conn.: Yale University Press.

Daniels, Belden and Kieschnick, Michael (1978). "Preliminary Research on Capital Markets and Economic Development." National Rural Center and the Opportunity Funding Corporation. National Rural Center. Nashville, Tenn.

Danielson, Michael N. (1976). *The Politics of Exclusion.* New York, N.Y.: Columbia University Press.

——, ed. (1971). *Metropolitan Politics: A Reader.* 2nd ed. Boston, Mass.: Little, Brown and Company.

Danielson, Michael N. and Doig, Jameson W. (1982). *Governing the New York Region.* Berkeley, Cal.: University of California Press.

Danielson, Michael N.; Hershey, Alan M.; and Bayne, John M. (1977). *One Nation, So Many Governments.* A report to the Ford Foundation. Lexington, Mass.: Lexington Books.

DeGrove, John M. and Stroud, Nancy (1981). "Local and Regional Governance Is the Changing Federalism of the 1980s." *American Federalism in the 1980s: Changes and Consequences.* Cambridge, Mass.: Lincoln Institute of Land Policy.

Derthick, Martha (1974). *Between State and Nation: Regional Organizations of the United States.* Washington, D.C.: The Brookings Institution.

DeTocqueville, Alexis (1838). *Democracy in America.* New York, N.Y.: G. Dearborn and Company.

Ditton, Robert B.; Seymour, John L.; and Swanson, Gerald C. (1977). *Coastal Resources Management.* Lexington, Mass.: Lexington Books.

Doig, Jameson W. (1966). *Metropolitan Transportation Politics.* New York, N.Y.: Columbia University Press.

Duke, Kathryn (1981). "At a Turning Point." Unpublished paper. Princeton, N.J.: Woodrow Wilson School of Public and International Affairs, Princeton University.

Duncan, Beverly and Lieberson, Stanley (1970). *Metropolis and Region in Transition*. Beverly Hills, Cal.: Sage Publications.

Duncan, Otis Dudley et al. (1960). *Metropolis and Region*. Baltimore, Md.: Johns Hopkins Press.

Edgmon, Terry D. (1979). "Areawide Environmental Management of Myth of the Region." *The Environmental Professional*, Vol. 1: 199–205.

Einsweiler, Robert (1977). "Thoughts About an Elected Versus Appointed Metropolitan Council." *Perspectives* 2.

Elazer, Daniel J. (1966). *American Federalism: A View from the States*. New York, N.Y.: Thomas T. Crowell.

Electric Power Research Institute (1980). *An Assessment of Oil Shale Technologies*.

Enthoven, Alvin C. and Freeman, Myrick A. III (1973). *Pollution, Resources and the Environment*. New York, N.Y.: W. W. Norton and Company.

Federal Register (1978). "Financial Assistance for Resource Recovery Project Development Under the President's Urban Policy." *Federal Register*, Vol. 43, No. 201. Washington, D.C.: U.S. Government Printing Office.

Fischer, John (1969). "The Minnesota Experiment: How to Make a Big City Fit to Live In." *Harper's*. Vol. 238, No. 427.

Florida Division of State Planning (1978). *Developments of Regional Impact, Summary of the First Five Years: July 1, 1973 through June 30, 1978*. Tallahassee, Fl.: Department of Administration, State of Florida.

Florida Office of Planning and Budgeting (1981). *Florida: Outlook for the 80's*. Tallahassee, Fl.: Executive Office of the Governor, State of Florida.

Friesema, H. Paul (1968). "The Metropolis and the Maze of Local Government." *New Urbanization*. Edited by Scott Greer et al. New York, N.Y.: St. Martin's Press.

—— (1970). "Interjurisdictional Agreements in Metropolitan Areas." *Administrative Science Quarterly*. Vol. 15, No. 2.

—— (1973). "Cities, Suburbs, and Short-Lived Models of Metropolitan Politics." *The Urbanization of the Suburbs*. Vol. 7 of *Urban Affairs Annual Reviews*. Edited by Louis H. Moasotti and Jeffrey K. Hadden. Beverly Hills, Cal.: Sage Publications.

Frisken, Francis (1973). "The Metropolis and the Central City: Can One Government Unite Them?" *Urban Affairs Quarterly*. Vol. 8, No. 3.

Gilje, Paul A. (1977). "Sharing of Tax Growth—Redefinitions." *Governmental Finance*. Municipal Finance Officers Association.

—— (1980). *Citizens League News*. Minneapolis, Minn.: The Citizens League.

Glendening and Atkins (1977). "The Politics of City-County Consolidation." *The County Yearbook*. Washington, D.C.: National Association of Counties.

Governors' Task Force on the Future of the Tri-State Regional Planning Commission (1981). *New Directions for Regional Planning: The New York-New Jersey-Connecticut Metropolitan Area*. New York, N.Y.: Tri-State Regional Planning Commission.

Graham, Robert (1981). *Remarks to the Statewide Regional Plannning Council Meeting*. Tallahassee, Fl.: Department of Veteran and Community Affairs, State of Florida.

Grant, Daniel R. (1964). "Metropolitics and Professional Political Leadership: The Case of Nashville." *Annals of the Academy of Political and Social Science.* Vol. 353.

—— (1965a). "A Comparison of Predictions and Experience with Nashville 'METRO'." *Urban Affairs Quarterly.* Vol. 1, No. 1.

—— (1965b). "Urban and Suburban Nashville: A Case Study in Metropolitanism." *The Journal of Politics.* Vol. 27, No. 1.

Greenstein, Fred I. and Wolfinger, Raymond E. (1958). "The Suburbs and Shifting Party Loyalties." *The Public Opinion Quarterly.* Vol. 22.

Greer, Scott (1962). *Governing the Metropolis.* New York, N.Y.: John Wiley and Sons.

—— (1963). *Metropolitics: A Study of Political Culture.* New York, N.Y.: John Wiley and Sons.

Gulick, Luther (1962). *The Metropolitan Problem and American Ideas.* New York, N.Y.: Alfred A. Knopf.

Haefle, E. T. (1973). *Representative Government and Environmental Management.* Washington, D.C.: Resources for the Future.

Hall, Peter (1970). *The Theory and Practice of Regional Planning.* London: Pemberton Books.

Hamilton, B. W. (1975). "Zoning and Property Taxation in a System of Local Governments." *Urban Studies.* Vol. 12.

Hand, Irving; McDowell, Bruce; and So, Frank, eds. (Forthcoming). *The Practice of State and Regional Planning.* Washington, D.C.: International City Management Association.

Harmon, Douglas B. (1969). "Councils of Government and Metropolitan Decision Making." *1969 Municipal Yearbook.*

Harrigan, John J. (1976). *Political Change in the Metropolis.* Boston, Mass.: Little, Brown and Company.

Harrigan, John J. and Johnson, William O. (1978). *Governing the Twin Cities Region: The Metropolitan Council in Comparative Perspective.* Minneapolis, Minn.: University of Minnesota Press.

Hartz, Louis (1955). *The Liberal Tradition in America.* New York, N.Y.: Harcourt, Brace and World.

Havard, William C. and Corty, Floyd C. (1964). *Rural-Urban Consolidation: The Merger of Governments in the Baton Rouge Area.* Baton Rouge: Louisiana State University Press.

Havley, Amos H. and Zimmer, Basil G. (1961). "Resistance to Unification in a Metropolitan Community." *Community Political Systems.* Edited by Morris Janowitz. Glencoe, Ill.: The Free Press.

—— (1970). *The Metropolitan Community: Its People and Government.* Beverly Hills, Cal.: Sage Publications.

Hawkins, Brett W. (1966). *Nashville Metro: The Politics of City-County Consolidation.* Nashville, Tenn.: Vanderbilt University Press.

Hawley, Willis (1970). *Black America's Stake in the Political Reorganization of Metropolitan Areas.* Berkeley, Cal.: Insitute of Governmental Studies, University of California.

—— (1972). *Blacks and Metropolitan Governance: The Stakes of Reform.* Berkeley, Cal.: Institute of Government Studies, University of California.

Hays, Forbes (1965). *Community Leadership: The Regional Plan Association of New York.* New York, N.Y.: Columbia University Press.

Heikoff, Joseph M. (1980). *Marine and Shoreland Resources Management.* Ann Arbor, Mich.: Ann Arbor Science Publishers.

Heller, Alfred, ed. (1971). *The California Tomorrow Plan.* Los Altos, Cal.: Uhlham Kaufman.

Henderson, Thomas A. and Rosenbaum, Walter A. (1973). "Prospects for Consolidation of Local Governments: The Role of Local Elites in Electoral Outcomes." *American Journal of Political Science.* Vol. 17, No. 4.

Herman, Harold (1963). *New York State and the Metropolitan Problem.* Philadelphia, Pa.: University of Pennsylvania Press.

Hill, Richard C. (1974). "Separate and Unequal: Governmental Inequality in the Metropolis." *The American Political Science Review.* Vol. 68, No. 4.

Hill, R. Steven and Mavam, William P. (1971). "Unigon: The First Year." *National Civic Review.* Vol. 6, No. 6.

Hirsch, Werner Z. (1968). "The Supply of Urban Public Services." *Issues in Urban Economics.* Edited by Harvey S. Perloff and Lowdon Wingo, Jr. Based on papers presented at a conference sponsored by the Committee on Urban Economics of Resources of the Future, Inc. Washington, D.C.: Johns Hopkins Press for Resources for the Future.

—— (1971). *Viability and Prospects for Metropolitan Leadership.* New York, N.Y.: Praeger Publishers.

Holden, Mathew Jr. (1964). "The Governance of the Metropolis as a Problem in Diplomacy." *Journal of Politics.* Vol. 26, No. 3.

Hoover, Edgar M. (1975). *An Introduction to Regional Economics.* 2nd ed. New York, N.Y.: Alfred A. Knopf.

Inwood, Ernest (1969). "Some Economic Aspects of a Proposed Bay Area Metropolitan Transportation Agency." *Annals of Regional Science.* Vol. 3, No. 2.

Jackson, Kenneth T. (1972). "Metropolitan Government Versus Suburban Autonomy: Politics on the Crabgrass Frontier." *Cities in American History.* Edited by Kenneth T. Jackson and Stanley K. Schultz. New York, N.Y.: Alfred A. Knopf.

Jones, Victor (1970). "Representative Local Government: From Neighborhood to Region." *Public Affairs Report.* Berkeley, Cal.: University of California.

Kain, John F. and Meyer, John R. (1971). *Essays in Regional Economics.* Cambridge, Mass.: Harvard University Press

Kaplan, Harold (1969). "Metro Toronto: Forming a Policy Formulation Process." *Urban Government.* Edited by Edward Banfield. New York, N.Y.: The Free Press.

Kegan, Lawrence, R. and Ronigen, George P. (1968). "The Outlook for State and Local Finance." *Fiscal Issues in the Future of Federalism.* New York, N.Y.: Committee for Economic Development.

Ketchum, Bostwick H., ed. (1972). *The Water's Edge: Critical Problems of the Coastal Zone.* Cambridge, Mass.: Massachusetts Institute of Technology Press.

Kinsey, David N. (1981). *Coastal Zone Management from the State Perspective: The New Jersey Experience, 1975-1980.* Cambridge, Mass.: The Lincoln Institute of Land Policy.

Knecht, Robert W. (1979) "Coastal Zone Management: The First Five Years and Beyond." *Coastal Zone Management Journal.* Vol. 6, No. 4.

Knudson, Edward (1976). *Regional Politics in the Twin Cities: A Report on the Politics and Planning of Urban Growth Policy.* St. Paul, Minn.: Metropolitan Council.

Kolderie, Ted and Gilje, Paul (1976). "The Citizens League Itself." *National Civic Review*, Vol. 65, No. 7.

Krefetz, Sharon P. and Sharof, Alan B. (1977). "City-County Merger Attempts: The Role of Political Factors." *National Civic Review*. Vol. 66, No. 4.

Landsberg, Hans H. and Schurr, Sam H. (1968). *Energy in the United States; Sources, Users, and Policy Issues*. New York, N.Y.: Random House.

Lang, Jean M., ed. (1975). *Resources and Decisions*. North Scituate, Mass.: Duxbury Press.

League of California Cities, Los Angeles County Division (1970). *Changing Role for Cities*. San Francisco, Cal.: League of California Cities.

Legislative History of the Coastal Zone Management Act of 1972, As Amended in 1974 and 1976 with a Section by Section Index. (December 1976). Washington, D.C.: U.S. Government Printing Office

Lerner, Michael A. (1981). "Coastal Mismanagement." *The New Republic*. (October 14).

Lichtenberg, Robert M. (1960). *One Tenth of a Nation*. Cambridge, Mass.: Harvard University Press for the Regional Plan Association.

MacCorkle, Stuart A. (1965). *Municipal Annexation in Texas*. Austin, Tex.: Institute of Public Affairs, University of Texas.

Marando, Vincent L. and Whitley, Carl Reggie. "City Council Consolidation: An Overview of Voter Response." *Urban Affairs Quarterly*. Vol. 8, No. 2.

Marshall, Dale (1970). *Metropolitan Government: Views of Minorities*. Washington, D.C.: Resources for the Future.

Matthewson, Kent, ed. (1978). *The Regionalist Papers*. 2nd ed. Detroit, Mich.: The Metropolitan Fund.

Maxey, Chester (1922). *National Municipal Review*.

McDowell, Bruce and Wright Carol. (1979). "The Fable of Regional Planning." *Public Management*. Vol. 61, No. 11.

Metropolitan Council (1977). *State of the Region: The Twin Cities Metropolitan Area*. St. Paul, Minn.: Metropolitan Council.

Meyerson, Martin E. (1956). "Building a Middle-Range Bridge for Comprehensive Planning." *Journal of American Institute of Planners*. Vol. 22, No. 1.

Mogulof, Melvin B. (1970). *Federal Regional Councils: Their Current Experience and Recommendations for Further Development*. Washington, D.C.: The Urban Institute.

—— (1971). *Governing Metropolitan Areas: A Critical Review of Councils of Governments and the Federal Role*. Washington, D.C.: The Urban Institute.

—— (1973). *Five Metropolitan Governments*. Washington, D.C.: The Urban Institute.

Murphy, Thomas (1970). *Metropolitics and the Urban County*. Washington, D.C.: Washington National Press.

Nash, William H. Jr. (1967). "The Effectiveness of Metropolitan Planning." *Taming Megalopolis: Vol. II, How to Manage an Urbanized World*. Edited by Wentworth Eldredge. Garden City, N.Y.: Doubleday and Company.

Nathan, Harriet and Scott, Stanley, eds. (1969). *Toward a Bay Area Regional Organization.* Berkeley, Cal.: Institute of Governmental Studies, University of California.

Nathan, R. (1981). *Background Material on Fiscal Year 1982 Federal Budget Reductions.* Princeton, N.J.: Princeton Urban and Regional Research Center, Princeton University.

National Association of Regional Councils (1979). *Regional Council Representation and Voting: A Guide to Issues and Alternatives.* Washington, D.C.: National Association of Regional Councils.

National Commission on Community Health (1966). *Health is a Community Affair.* Washington, od.C.: U.S. Government Printing Office.

National Municipal League (1909). *Proceedings of the Cincinnati Conference for Good City Government.* New York, N.Y.: National Municipal League.

—— (1930). *The Government of Metropolitan Areas in the United States.* New York, N.Y.: National Municipal League

—— (1955). *Model State and Regional Planning Law.* New York, N.Y.: National Municipal League.

National Service to Regional Councils (1970). Memorandum on "Regional Council Trends." Washington, D.C. Mimeographed.

New Jersey County and Municipal Government Study Commission (1968). *Creative Localism: A Perspective.* Trenton, N.J.: New Jersey County and Municipal Government Study Commission.

—— (1981). *The Impacts of Mandates on Counties.* Trenton, N.J.: New Jersey County and Municipal Government Study Commission.

New Jersey Department of Environmental Protection, Division of Coastal Resources, (1980). *New Jersey Coastal Management Program and Final Environmental Impact Statement.* Trenton, N. J.: New Jersey Department of Environmental Protection.

New York Joint Legislative Committee on Metropolitan and Regional Study (1967). *Governing Urban Areas: Realism and Reform.* Albany, N.Y.: New York Joint Legislative Committee on Metropolitan and Regional Study.

Norton, James A. (1963). *The Metro Experience.* Cleveland, Oh.: The Press of Western Reserve University.

Ostrom, Vincent; Tiebout, Charles M.; and Warren, Robert (1961). "Organizing Government in Metropolitan Areas: A Theoretical Inquiry." *American Political Science Review.* Vol. 55, No. 4.

Peat, Marwick, and Mitchell (1981). *Tri-State Financial Management System Review and Implementation Plan.* Report prepared for the Tri-State Regional Planning Commission.

Perloff, Harvey S. et al. (1960). *Regions, Resources and Economic Growth.* Baltimore, Md.: Johns Hopkins Press.

Peterson, George E. (1976). "Finance." *The Urban Predicament.* Edited by William Gorham and Nathan Glazer. Washington, D.C.: The Urban Institute.

President of the United States (1981). *America's New Beginning: A Program for Economic Recovery.* Washington, D.C.: The White House.

President's Commission on National Goals (1960). *Goals for Americans.* Englewood Cliffs, N.J.: Prentice-Hall.

Ranney, David C. (1969). *Planning and Politics in the Metropolis.* Columbus, Oh.: Merrill Publishing Company.

Reagan, Michael D. (1972). *The New Federalism.* New York, N.Y.: Oxford University Press.

Reed, B. J. (1981). "States Bring Local Officials into Block Grant Plans." *Nation's Cities Weekly.*

Reed, Thomas H. (1941). "The Metropolitan Problem—1941." *National Municipal Review.* Vol. 30, No. 7.

—— (1950). "Hope for Suburbanitis." *National Municipal Review.* Vol. 39, No. 11.

Reichert, Peggy (1976). *Growth Management in the Twin Cities Metropolitan Area: A Report for Planners on the Development Framework Planning Process.* St. Paul, Minn.: The Metropolitan Council.

Reid, J. N. and Stam, J. M. (1982). "Funding Cuts Hit Substate Regions." *Public Administration Times.*

Resource Management Task Force (1980). *Final Report to Governor Graham.* Tallahassee, Fl.: Executive Office of the Governor, State of Florida.

Rothenberg, Jerome (1970). "Local Decentralization and the Theory Of Optimal Government." *The Analysis of Public Output.* Edited by Julius Margolis. New York, N.Y.: Columbia University Press.

Scheiber, Walter (1969). "Evolution of a COG: Tackling the Tough Jobs." *Public Management.*

Schmandt, Henry J.; Steinbicker, P. G.; and Wendel, G. D. (1961). *Metropolitan Reform in St. Louis.* New York, N.Y.: Holt, Rinehart and Winston.

Schoop, E. Jack and Hirten, John E. (1971). "The San Francisco Bay Plan: Combining Policy with Police Power." *Journal of the American Institute of Planners.* Vol. 37, No. 1.

Schurr, Sam and Retschert, Bruce (1977). *Energy in the American Economy: 1850 - 1975.* Baltimore, Md.: Johns Hopkins University Press.

Scott, Stanley and Bollens, John (1980). *Governing a Metropolitan Region: The San Francisco Bay Area.* Berkeley, Cal.: Institute of Governmental Studies, University of California.

Scott, Stanley and Corzine, John (1962). *Special Districts in the San Francisco Bay Area: Some Problems and Issues.* Berkeley, Cal.: The Institute of Government Studies, University of California.

Shelton, Donn (1972). *Regional Citizenship.* Detroit, Mich.: Metropolitan Fund, Inc.

Shore, William B. (1967). *Public Participation in Regional Planning.* New York, N.Y.: Regional Plan Association.

—— (1974). *Listening to the Metropolis.* New York, N.Y.: Regional Plan Association.

Siebert, Horst (1969). *Regional Economic Growth: Theory and Policy.* Scranton, Pa.: International Textbook Company.

Sloan, Alfred P., Jr. (1973). *My Years with General Motors.* New York, N.Y.: Doubleday and Company.

Sloan, Lee and French, Robert (1970). "Race and Governmental Consolidation in Jacksonville." *Negro Educational Review.* Vol. 21, Nos. 2-3.

Smallwood, Frank (1963). *Metro Toronto: A Decade Later.* Toronto, Canada: Bureau of Municipal Research.

—— (1965). *Greater London: The Politics of Metropolitan Reform.* Indianapolis, Ind.: Bobbs-Merrill.

Smith, Robert W. (1969). *Public Authorities in Urban Areas.* Washington, D.C.: National Association of Counties.

Sofen, Edward (1963). *The Miami Metropolitan Experiment.* Bloomington, Ind.: Indiana University Press.

Sorensen, Jens (1979). "State-Local Relations in Coastal Zone Management: Implications for Change." *Coastal Zone Management Journal,* Vol. 6, No. 4.

Sparlin, Estal E. (1960). "Cleveland Seeks New Metro Solution." *National Civic Review,* Vol. 69, No. 3 (March): 143.

Stam, Jerome M. and Reid, J. Norman (1980). *Federal Programs Supporting Multicounty Substate Regional Activities: An Overview.* Rural Development Research Report No. 23. Washington, D.C.: U.S. Department of Agriculture, Economics, Statistics and Cooperative Service.

Stanley Consultants (1976). *Resource Recovery from Municipal Solid Waste in Ohio.* Columbus, Oh.: Ohio Environmental Protection Agency, State of Ohio.

—— (1978). *Resource Recovery from Municipal Solid Waste in Cuyahoga County.* Columbus, Oh.: Ohio Environmental Protection Agency, State of Ohio.

Starnes, Earl M. (1981). *New Initiatives for Regional Planning in Florida.* Gainesville, Fl.

Starr, Roger (1969). "Power and Powerlessness in a Regional City." *The Public Interest.* Vol. 16, (Summer): 10.

Stobaugh, Robert and Yergin, Daniel, eds. (1979). *Energy Future: Report of the Energy Project at the Harvard Business School.* New York, N.Y.: Random House.

Subcommittee on Urban Affairs, Joint Economic Committee (1971). *Regional Planning.* Hearings, 92nd Congress. Washington, D.C.: U.S. Government Printing Office.

Sundquist, James L. (1969). *Making Federalism Work.* Washington, D.C.: The Brookings Institution.

Tiebout, Charles M. (1956). "A Pure Theory of Local Expenditures." *Journal of Political Economy.* Vol. 64, No. 5.

U.S. Bureau of the Budget (1969). *Circular A-95.* Washington, D.C.: U.S. Government Printing Office.

U.S. Bureau of the Census (1970). *Journey To Work, 1970.* Washington, D.C.: U.S. Government Printing Office.

—— (1978). *Regional Organizations,* Vol. 6, No. 6, 1977 Census of Governments. Washington, D.C.: U.S. Government Printing Office.

U.S. Commission on Intergovernmental Relations (The Kestnbaum Commission) (1955). *Report to the President.* Washington, D.C.: U.S. Government Printing Office.

U.S. Commission on Marine Science, Engineering and Resources (The Stratton Commission) (1969). *Science and Environment.* Vol. 1 of the Panel Reports of the Commission on Marine Science, Engineering and Resources. Washington, D.C.: U.S. Government Printing Office.

U.S. Congressional Research Service (1977). *National Energy Transportation.* Vol. 1. Washington, D.C.: U.S. Government Printing Office.

—— (1979). *Centralized vs. Decentralized Energy Systems.* Washington, D.C.: U.S. Government Printing Office.

U.S. Department of Housing and Urban Development (1970). *Areawide Planning Requirements.* Washington, D.C.: U.S. Government Printing Office.

—— (1980). *Metropolitan Governance: A Handbook for Local Government Study Commissions.* Washington, D.C.: U.S. Government Printing Office.

U.S. Department of Transportation (1981). *A Directory of Regularly Scheduled, Fixed Route, Local Public Transportation Service in Urbanized Areas Over 50,000 Population.* Urban Mass Transportation Administration, Office of Planning, Management and Demonstration. Washington, D.C.: U.S. Government Printing Office.

U.S. Department of Energy, Energy Information Administration (1980). *Monthly Energy Review.* Washington, D.C.: U.S. Government Printing Office.

U.S. Environmental Protection Agency (1976). *Impacts of Construction Activities in Wetlands of the United States.* EPA-600/3-76-045. Corvallis, Ore.

U.S. Office of Management and Budget, Intergovernmental Affairs Division (1980). *Conceptual Outline of Proposed Revisions of OMB Circular A-95.* Washington, D.C.: Office of Management and Budget.

—— (1981). "Standard Metropolitan Statistical Areas and Standard Consolidated Statistical Areas." *Statistical Reporter.* Washington, D.C.: U.S. Government Printing Office.

U.S. Office of Technology Assessment (1976). *An Assessment of Community Planning for Mass Transit.* Prepared by Skidmore, Owings and Merrill Systems Design Concepts. (OTA-T-16). Washington, D.C.: U.S. Government Printing Office.

U.S. Office of Technology Assessment (1978). *An Assessment of Oil Shale Technologies.* Washington, D.C.: U.S. Government Printing Office.

U.S. Senate Subcommittee on Intergovernmental Relations (1964). *The Effectiveness of Metropolitan Planning.* Study conducted by the Joint Center for Urban Studies, Massachusetts Institute of Technology and Harvard University. Washington, D.C.: U.S. Government Printing Office.

U.S. Task Force on Planning Assistance (1969). *A Federal Planning Assistance Strategy.*

Walsh, Anne Marie (1978). *The Public's Business.* Cambridge, Mass.: Massachusetts Institute of Technology Press.

Wilson, James Q. (1968). *The Metropolitan Enigma.* Cambridge, Mass.: Harvard University Press.

—— (1981). *The Public Interest.* (Summer) 1981.

Wilson, Thomas (1964). *Policies for Regional Development.* University of Glascow, Social and Economic Studies, Occasional Paper No. 3. Edinburgh and London: Oliver and Boyd.

Wingo, Lowden (1972). *Reform of Metropolitan Governments.* Washington, D.C.: Resources for the Future.

Wirt, Frederick M. et al. (1972). *On the City's Rim: Politics and Policy in Suburbia.* Lexington, Mass.: D. C. Heath.

Wise, Harold (1971). *Recommendations for Action on Multi-County Governmental Organization.* Washington, D.C. (Mimeographed).

Wood, Robert C. (1961). *1400 Governments: The Political Economy of the New York Metropolitan Region.* Cambridge, Mass.: Harvard University Press.

Wright, Deil S. (1974). "Intergovernmental Relations: An Analytic Overview." *Annals of the American Academy of Political and Social Science.* Vol. 416.

Ylvesaker, Paul N. (1968). "The Growing Role of State Governments in Local Affairs." *State Government.* Vol. 61, No. 2.

Zeller, Florence (1978). *Intergovernmental Relations: A Handbook for Local Officials.* Washington, D.C.: National Association of Counties/International City Management Association.

Zimmerman, Joseph F. (1970). "Metropolitan Reform in the U.S.: An Overview." *Public Administration Review.* Vol. 30, No. 5.

—— (1972). "Substates Regional Government: Designing a New Procedure." *National Civic Review.* Vol. 61, No. 6.

Index

About the Contributors

GILL C. LIM is an Assistant Professor of Public and International Affairs at Princeton University. He has previously taught at Northwestern University and served as a consultant to the World Bank and national and local planning agencies.

WILLIAM N. CASSELLA, JR. is the Executive Director of the Citizens Forum on Self-Government/ National Municipal League, Inc. in New York City. Formerly he was a research associate for the Government Affairs Foundation and for the Metropolitan Region Program, Columbia University. He is a consultant to the Advisory Commission on Intergovernmental Relations, and Chairman of the Westchester County (N.Y.) Planning Board.

BRUCE D. McDOWELL currently is a senior analyst with the Advisory Commission on Intergovernmental Relations. He has held several posts with the Metropolitan Washington Council of Governments and was a senior planner for the Maryland-National Capital Park and Planning Commission.

PATRICK J. HOLLAND is the Assistant Director of the Cuyahoga County Sanitary Engineering Department's Resource Recovery Program in Cleveland, Ohio. Mr. Holland's previous experience includes political consulting with specialization in fiscal management and fund raising.

ALDEN McLELLAN, IV is the Assistant Commissioner for Science and Research of the New Jersey Department of Environmental Protection. A registered Professional Engineer, he served at the Technical-Scientific University of Tehran, Iran, and was head of the Environmental Engineering Division of the Iranian Nuclear Energy Company for three years. He is the president-elect of the New Jersey Academy of Science.

BRIAN D. BOXER is an urban and regional planner specializing in land-use and environmental issues. He recently completed advanced study in public affairs and urban planning at Princeton University's Woodrow Wilson School of Public and International Affairs. He has served with the California Coastal Commission and has researched and written on aspects of urban, regional, and environmental planning.

ROGER VAUGHAN is the Deputy Director of the State of New York Office of Development Planning. He has held positions as an Assistant Vice President of Citibank researching New York City development, as an economist for the Rand Corporation, and has taught at the Graduate School of Public Administration, New York University.

JACK V. BOYD is currently the Director of Oklahoma's Health Planning Program. He began his public service career as Executive Director of the Oklahoma Planning and Resources Board and has also served as the Director of the Oklahoma State Legislative Council Committee on Rehabilitation Services. He received the 1981 National Schlesinger Achievement Award in Health Planning.

RICHARD S. PAGE is the General Manager of the Washington Metropolitan Area Transit Authority. Formerly he served as Administrator of the U.S. Department of Transportation's Urban Mass Transportation program, as executive director of the Seattle Metropolitan Transit System, and as Deputy Mayor of Seattle.

TED KOLDERIE is a Senior Fellow at the Hubert H. Humphrey Institute of Public Affairs, University of Minnesota. He has participated in the White House Conference on National Growth and Urban Development of 1978, and has been an American Political Science Association Congressional Fellow.

INGRID W. REED is the Assistant Dean for Planning and Administration of the Woodrow Wilson School at Princeton University. Ms. Reed is the Chair of the Mercer County (N.J.) Planning Board and has served on the Task Force on the Future of the Tri-State Planning Commission.

DENTON U. KENT most currently served as the Chief Administrative Officer of the Portland Metropolitan Service District. He received the 1979 National Association of Regional Councils Intergovernmental Leadership Award, is a member of the National Urban Policy Round Table, and is an active member of the International City Managers Association. He has served as a consultant to local governments both on the national and international level.

NANCY ELLEN STROUD is a regional planner and lawyer currently associated with the law firm of Ross, Hardies, O'Keefe, Babcock, and Parsons in Boca Raton, Florida. Ms. Stroud advises regional planning councils in Florida on growth management and has served on the Governor's Resource Management Task Force to improve Florida's growth management laws.

CHARLES R. WARREN is a Senior Research Associate at the National Academy of Public Administration. He was consultant to the Special Assistant to the President for Information Systems and Staff Assistant, Office of Public Liaison in the White House during 1978–80, and has been Urban Policy Advisor in the U.S. Department of Commerce.